英汉对照·心灵阅读（一）

Experiences
人生篇

许兰贞　编译

外文出版社

卷首语

总有一种感动无处不在。

总有一种情怀轻舞飞扬。

总有一种生活,在别处,闪动异样的光芒。

阅读,让我们的生活在情调与知性中享受更多……

故事与见闻,犹如生活的魅力与智慧,合着我们自身生命的光与影,陪伴我们一路前行。

快乐和圆满,幻想与失落,飞扬的眼泪,

行走江湖的落拓，不与人说的痛苦，渐行渐远的繁华，坚持的勇气，点点滴滴的小意思……

人生让我们感受到的，也许远远不只是这些；更多的是挫折后生长的力量，沉闷时的豁然开朗，是屋前那静静的南山上盛开的人淡如菊的境界，是闹市中跋涉红尘、豪情万丈的冲动，是很纯粹的一杯午后的香醇的咖啡……

漫步红尘，有彻悟来自他人的故事，有灵犀来自偶然的相遇，在这里，一种从未见过的却可能早就在我们心底的生活方式有可能与我们邂逅。

让我们一起阅读吧，感受生长的智慧、风雅与力量。

Contents
目　　录

1. The art of living　/　1

 生活的艺术

2. How to be true to yourself　/　9

 怎样做一个表里如一的人

3. The value of friendship　/　17

 友谊的价值

4. A simple truth about happiness　/　25

 快乐真言

5. To be a better friend　/　35

 做个更好的朋友

6. Every day is a gift from God　/　43

 每一天都是上帝赐予的礼物

7. A dance with Dad　/　51

 和父亲共舞

8. A daughter thanks her mother　/　61

 女儿对母亲的感谢

9. Books / 69

　　书籍

10. Tips for staying calm / 77

　　保持平静的秘诀

11. The little words that work marriage magic / 87

　　创造婚姻奇迹的小小字眼

12. Love is not merchandise / 93

　　爱情不是商品

13. We are raising children, not flowers! / 99

　　我们是在抚养孩子,不是在养花!

14. Establish a sound relationship with your body / 103

　　珍爱你的身体

15. Please dress me in red / 111

　　请给我穿上红色的衣服

16. Sand and stone / 117

　　伤害只写在沙地上

17. A full-time school called life / 123

　　生活是一所全日制学校

18. There are no mistakes, only lessons / 129

　　没有错误,只有教训

19. Win-win contract / 135
　　双赢的协定

20. Mule in the well / 141
　　井底之骡

21. The richest woman in the world / 147
　　世上最富有的女人

22. "There" is no better than "here" / 155
　　彼岸无尽头,知足才常乐

23. Two frogs / 161
　　两只青蛙

24. Others are only mirrors of you / 165
　　别人其实是你的一面镜子

25. No scorecard in marriage / 171
　　婚姻生活中不需要记分卡

26. All about love / 177
　　关于恋情

27. Relax / 183
　　休息放松

28. What you make of your life is up to you / 189
　　生活全由你自己去创造

29. Food for thought   /   197
   精神食粮

30. Support   /   203
   支持

31. On the shoulders of a hero   /   209
   坐在勇士的肩膀上

32. The chain of love   /   219
   爱的延续

33. Those strangers we know   /   229
   熟悉的陌生人

34. Paradox of our times   /   237
   我们这个时代的尴尬

35. The Teddy Stoddard's story   /   243
   泰迪·斯托达德的故事

36. Choose optimism   /   253
   选择乐观

37. The wholeness of life   /   261
   健全的人生

The art of living
生活的艺术

A man comes to this world with his fist clenched, but, when he dies, his hand is open.

一个人来到世上时,手是紧握成拳的,但离开这个世界时,他的手是张开的。

人生篇

The art of living is to know when to hold fast and when to let go. For life is a paradox[1]: it enjoins[2] us to cling to its many gifts even while it ordains[3] their eventual relinquishment[4]. The rabbis[5] of old put it this way: "A man comes to this world with his fist clenched, but, when he dies, his hand is open."

Surely we ought to hold fast to life, for it is wondrous and full of a beauty. We know that this is so, but all too often we recognize this truth only in our backward glance when we remember what was, and then suddenly realize that it is no more.

We remember a beauty that faded, a love that waned. But, we remember with far greater pain that we did not see that beauty when it flowered, that we failed to respond with love when it was tendered.

A recent experience re-taught me this truth. I was hospitalized following a severe heart attack and had been in intensive care for several days. It was not a pleasant place.

One morning, I had to have some additional tests. The required machines were located in a building at the opposite end of the hospital, so I had to be wheeled across the courtyard on a gurney[6].

As we emerged from our unit, the sunlight hit me. That's all there was to my experience. Just the light of the sun. And yet how beautiful it was how warming, how sparking, how brilliant! I

生活的艺术

生活的艺术是要懂得取舍。因为生活本身就是一个矛盾：它一边告诫我们要珍惜它所赋予的一切，一边又注定最后它要将其全部收回。古时犹太教的教士们这样说："一个人来到世上时，手是紧握成拳的，但离开这个世界时，他的手是张开的。"

我们当然应该牢牢抓住生活，因为它奇妙、富有美感。我们明白这一点，但是往往只是在我们蓦然回首忆及往事，然后突然意识到好景不再，才会对此深有体会。

我们记得已经凋零的美，已经消逝的爱。但是我们却痛苦地忆起，我们没有在美丽绽放的时候看到那份美丽，没有在爱意绵绵时以爱回应。

我最近的一次经历再次让我认识到这个真理。一次严重的心脏病发作后，我住进了医院，在特护区住了好几天。这可不是什么令人愉快的地方。

一天早上，我得再做一些检查，检查所需的器械在医院对面尽头的一座大楼里，因此，我必须躺在轮床上被人推着从院子里经过。

我们从病房里出来的时候，阳光照在我的身上。这就是我当时的感受，只不过是阳光嘛。但是那阳光多美啊——那么温暖，那

---

❶ **paradox**
/'pærədɒks/
n. 自相矛盾的人或物

❷ **enjoin**
/ɪn'dʒɔɪn/
vt. (formal) 命令

❸ **ordain**
/ɔː'deɪn/
vt. 命令，决定

❹ **relinquishment**
/rɪ'lɪŋkwɪʃmənt/
n. 放弃，让与

❺ **rabbi**
/'ræbaɪ/
n. 犹太教的教士

❻ **gurney**
/'ɡɜːnɪ/
n. 轮床

looked to see whether anyone else relished[7] the sun's golden glow, but everyone was hurrying to and fro, most with eyes fixed on the ground. Then I remembered how often I, too, have been indifferent to the grandeur of each day, too preoccupied with petty and sometimes even meaningless concerns. At that moment, I came to realize life's gifts are precious — but we are too heedless of[8] them.

Here then is the first pole of life's paradoxical demands on us : Never too busy for the wonder and the awe of life. Be reverent[9] before each dawning day. Embrace each hour. Seize each golden minute.

Hold fast to life, but not so fast that you cannot let go. This is the second side of life's coin, the opposite pole of its paradox: we must accept our losses, and learn how to let go.

This is not an easy lesson to learn, especially when we are young and think that the world is ours to command, that whatever we desire with the full force of our passionate being can, nay, will, be ours. But then life moves along to confront with realities, and slowly but surely this truth dawns upon us.

At every stage of life we sustain losses — and grow in the process. We begin our independent lives only when we emerge from the womb and lose its protective shelter. We enter a progression of schools, then we leave our mothers and fathers and our childhood homes. We get married and have children and

么耀眼，那么灿烂！我环顾四周，想看看是不是还有人在欣赏这金灿灿的阳光，但是所有人都行色匆匆，大都是眼睛盯着地面。这时，我想起了对于每天的阳光我也是经常无动于衷，只关注于那些琐碎甚至是无意义的小事。就在那一刻，我突然意识到生活的礼物是珍贵的——但是我们却忽视了它们。

那么，这就是生活对于我们自相矛盾的要求的一极：永远不要因为过于忙碌而忽略了生活的奇妙、威严。要对到来的每一天充满敬意。拥抱每一个小时；抓住宝贵的每一分钟。

抓住生活，但不要抓得太紧，以致于无法放弃。这是生活像钱币似的另一面，也是其矛盾的另一极：我们必须接受失去，并学会放弃。

要学会这一课并不容易，尤其是当我们年轻气盛的时候。因为，那时我们认为自己是世界的主宰，认为我们用充满激情的躯体中的全部力量去渴求的东西终将是我们的。但是，随后而来的生活将现实摆到了我们的面前，我们才慢慢地明白了这个道理。

在人生的每一阶段我们都会有所失——并在此过程中成长。我们只有在离开母体失去其庇护时才开始独立的生活。我们进入各级学

❼ **relish**
/'relɪʃ/
vt. 欣赏；享受

❽ **heedless of**
忽视，不注意

❾ **reverent**
/'revərənt/
n. 恭敬的

then have to let them go. We confront the death of our parents and our spouses. We face the gradual or not so gradual waning of our strength. And ultimately, as the parable of the open and closed hand suggests, we must confront the inevitability of our own demise[10], losing ourselves as it were, all that we were or dreamed to be.

校，然后离开父母，离开了我们孩提时代生活过的故乡。我们结婚生子，然后再放飞子女。我们要面对父母和配偶的死亡。我们逐渐或许很快变得越来越衰弱。最终，就像张开和闭合的手一样，我们必须面对自身的死亡，失去原有的自我，失去我们所有的一切或是我们所梦想的一切。

❿ **demise**
/dɪˈmaɪz/
n. 死亡

How to be true to yourself
怎样做一个表里如一的人

Life is like a field of newly fallen snow; where I choose to walk every step will show.

生活好像一片刚刚落满白雪的土地；我走到哪里，我的每一个脚印就会出现在哪里。

My grandparents believed you were either honest or you weren't. There was no in between. They had a simple motto hanging on their living-room wall: "Life is like a field of newly fallen snow; where I choose to walk every step will show." They didn't have to talk about it—they demonstrated the motto by the way they lived.

They understood instinctively that integrity means having a personal standard of morality and ethics that does not <u>sell out</u>[1] to expediency[2] and that is not relative to the situation at hand. Integrity is an inner standard for judging your behavior. Unfortunately, integrity is in short supply today—and getting scarcer. But it is the real bottom line in every area of society. And it is something we must demand of ourselves.

A good test for this value is to look at what I call the Integrity Triad, which consists of three key principles:

1. *Stand firmly for your convictions[3] in the face of personal pressure*. There's a story told about a surgical nurse's first day on the medical team at a well-known hospital. She was responsible for ensuring that all instruments and materials were accounted for during an abdominal[4] operation. The nurse said to the surgeon, "You've only removed 11 sponges, and we used 12. We need to find the last one."

"I removed them all," the doctor declared. "We'll close now."

怎样做一个表里如一的人

我的爷爷和奶奶认为，你要么是诚实的，要么不是。不可能介于两者之间。在他们起居室的墙上挂着一幅简单易懂的座右铭："生活好像一片刚刚落满白雪的土地；我走到哪里，我的每一个脚印就会出现在哪里。"他们无需就此加以评说——他们是以身体力行的方式来证实这幅座右铭的。

他们本能的理解是，诚实意味着具备一定的伦理道德标准，既不看风使舵，也不随着眼下的形势而转移。诚实是判断你行为的内在标准。遗憾的是，如今，诚实处在短缺状态——甚至越来越稀罕。然而，它却是社会各个领域真正的思想上的底线，而且是我们必须要求自己严格做到的。

我所谓的诚实三要素是检验这种价值标准的一个有效方法，其中包括三条主要原则：

1. 在个人压力面前，要坚定信念。 有一个关于一位外科护士在一所著名医院的医疗组第一天上班时发生的故事。在一个腹部手术中，她负责清点所有使用的器材。这位护士对外科医生说："我们用了12块纱布，而你却只取出了11块。我们必须找到最后那一块。"

"我全都取出来了，"那位医生肯定地说。"我们现在缝上刀口吧。"

❶ **sell out**
出卖，背叛
❷ **expediency**
/ɪk'spiːdɪənsɪ/
n. 权宜之计，应急手段
❸ **conviction**
/kən'vɪkʃn/
n. 信念；信服
❹ **abdominal**
/æb'dɒmɪnəl/
adj. 腹部的

"You can't do that, sir," objected the rookie[5] nurse. "Think of the patient."

Smiling, the surgeon lifted his foot and showed the nurse the 12th sponge.

"You'll do just fine in this or any other hospital," he told her.

When you know you're right, you can't back down[6].

2. *Always give others credit that is rightfully theirs.* Don't be afraid of those who might have a better idea or who might even be smarter than you are.

David Ogilvy, founder of the advertising firm Ogilvy & Mather, made this point clear to his newly appointed office heads by sending each a Russian nesting doll with five progressively smaller figures inside.

His message was contained in the smallest doll: "If each of us hires people who are smaller than we are, we shall become a company of dwarfs. But if each of us hires people who are bigger than we are, Ogilvy & Mather will become a company of giants." And that is precisely what the company became — one of the largest and most respected advertising organizations in the world.

3. *Be honest and open about who you really are.* People who lack genuine core values rely on external factors — their looks or

"先生，您不能那么办，"这位新来的护士反驳道。"要为病人着想。"

外科医生笑着抬起脚，让护士看到了第12块纱布。"不管在这所医院，还是在其他任何医院，你都会干得非常出色，"他称赞这位护士说。

当你知道你做得对的时候，你就不能退缩。

2. 对那些值得赞扬的人要常常给予肯定。切莫害怕那些可能有更好主意的或者那些可能比你更聪明的人。

奥格尔维和马瑟广告公司的创建人戴维·奥格尔维，通过送给他新任命的部门经理每人一套俄罗斯风格的套叠式玩具娃娃（里面共有5个依次变小的玩具娃娃）而把这一点清楚地告诉了他们。

在最小的玩具娃娃里面，有戴维的留言："如果我们每个人所雇用的人比我们个子小，我们的公司就会成为矮子公司。反之，如果我们每个人所雇用的人比我们个子大，那么，奥格尔维和马瑟将会成为一个巨人公司。而这正是那家公司发展的结果——它终于成为世界上最大、最有声望的广告公司之一。

3. 真诚、坦率地展示真实的你。那些缺乏真正的基本价值观念的人，为了使自己感

❺ rookie
/ˈrʊkɪ/
adj. (informal) 新来的，新上任的
❻ back down
退缩，后退

status—in order to feel good about themselves. Inevitably they will do everything they can to preserve this facade[7], but they will do very little to develop their inner value and personal growth.

So be yourself. Don't engage in a personal cover-up of areas that are unpleasing in your life. When it's tough, do it tough. In other words, face reality and be adult in your responses to life's challenges.

觉良好而依靠外在因素——相貌或社会地位。他们势必尽一切可能来保全这种表面形象，却很少会去培养自己内在的价值和注重个人的成长。

因此，要展示你的真面目。不要设法掩饰你生活中令人不快的方方面面。艰难时刻要顽强。换言之，要正视现实。面对生活的挑战，要老成持重，应付有方。

7 facade
/fə'sɑːd/
n. (虚伪的) 外表

The value of friendship
友谊的价值

Very close and trusted friends share confidences candidly.

亲密而互相信任的朋友，他们彼此赤诚相待。

Friendship is both a source of pleasure and a component of good health. People who have close friends naturally enjoy their company. Of equal importance are the concrete emotional benefits they derive. When something sensational[1] happens to us, sharing the happiness of the occasion with friends intensifies our joy. Conversely, in times of trouble and tension, when our spirits are low, unburdening our worries and fears to compassionate friends alleviates[2] the stress. Moreover, we may even get some practical suggestions for solving a particular problem.

From time to time, we are insensitive and behave in a way that hurts someone's feelings. Afterward, when we feel guilty and down in the dumps[3], friends can reassure us. This positive interaction is therapeutic[4], and much less expensive than visits so a psychologist.

Throughout life, we rely on small groups of people for love, admiration, respect, moral support, and help. Almost everyone has a "network" of friends: co-workers, neighbors, and schoolmates. While both men and women have such friends, evidence is accumulating that indicates men rarely make close friends. Men are sociable and frequently have numerous business acquaintances, golf buddies, and so on. However, friendship does not merely involve a sharing of activities; it is a sharing of self on a very personal level. Customarily, men have shied away from close relationships in which they confide in[5] others. By bottling up[6] their emotions, men deprive themselves of a healthy outlet for their negative feelings.

友谊既是快乐的源泉，又是健康的一个组成部分。有挚交者自然喜欢与其挚友为伴，因为他们在精神上可得到快乐。每逢喜事就与朋友分享可谓喜上加喜。反之，在不如意时，情绪低沉，向富有同情心的朋友倾诉衷肠，会减轻痛苦。此外，我们甚至还可以得到一些实际的建议去解决某一个别问题。

有时我们对他人麻木不仁，甚至行为中不知不觉伤害了他人的感情。事后我们感到愧疚和沮丧，这时朋友会安慰我们。这种积极的双向行为犹如一剂良药，远远比求助于心理学家合算。

我们在一生中都有赖于一些小团体来获得友爱、赏识、尊重、道义上的支持和帮助。几乎人人都有一个"友谊网"：同事、邻居和同学。尽管男人和女人都有这样一些朋友，但越来越多的迹象表明，男人不容易交上挚友。男子喜欢社交，常与大批同仁、高尔夫球友等人交往。然而，友谊不仅包括参与活动，也包括在纯粹私人的范围内分享对方的一切。在一般情况下，男人总是避开那种可以向对方交心的亲密关系。男人因为掩盖自己的情感而丧失了抒发消极情绪的健康途径。

正因为友谊可以提高我们的生活质量，

❶ sensational
/sen'seɪʃənl/
adj. 了不起的，很好的

❷ alleviate
/ə'liːvɪeɪt/
vt. 减轻；缓和

❸ down in the dumps
神情沮丧的

❹ therapeutic
/ˌθerə'pjuːtɪk/
adj. 治疗的

❺ confide in
信任；吐露秘密

❻ bottle up
掩盖；抑制

Because friendships enhance our lives, it is important to cultivate them. Unfortunately, it is somewhat difficult to make long-lasting close friends. People are mobile, and mobility puts a strain on friendships. Long distances between friends discourage intimacy. Long distance telephone conversations are costly, and letter writing is not a deeply ingrained habit. Divorce is also destructive to friendship. In many cases, when divorce occurs, friendships disintegrate because couples usually prefer to associate with other couples.

People choose some friends because they are fun to be with; they "make things happen". Likewise, common interests appear to be a significant factor in selecting friends. Families with children, for instance, tend to gravitate[7] toward families with children. It is normal to be friend people who have similar lifestyles and it is perfectly acceptable to select friends for special qualities as long as there is a balanced giving and taking that is mutually satisfying.

Very close and trusted friends share confidences candidly[8]. They feel secure that they will not be ridiculed[9] or derided[10], and their confidences will be honored. Betraying a trust is a very quick and painful way to terminate a friendship.

As friendships solidify[11], ties strengthen. Intimate relationships enrich people's lives. Some components of a thriving friendship are honesty, naturalness, thoughtfulness and some common interests.

所以我们应高度重视它。遗憾的是，要交经得起时间考验的挚友尤其困难。人总免不了走南闯北，这种动荡不定时刻考验着友情。人走茶凉便是这个道理。长途电话打不起，至于写信，许多人天生就不爱写信。离婚也会毁灭友爱，因为在大多数情况下，夫妻一旦分手，友谊便随之土崩瓦解，因为已婚夫妇通常都更愿意与其他夫妻交往。

人们择友，有时因为情趣相投。朋友使你的生活生机勃勃。同样，共同的兴趣是择友的一个重要因素。例如，有孩子的家庭之间容易相互吸引。生活方式相似的人互相交友也是正常的。选择有特性的人交友，这是无可厚非的，只要给予与索取保持平衡，双方皆感满意。

亲密而互相信任的朋友，他们彼此赤诚相待。他们不会互相戏弄和嘲笑，因而心里踏实自在。他们之间的这种信任也会受到旁人的尊重。背信弃义则会迅速而痛苦地断送友谊。

随着友谊的日益巩固，友谊的纽带也更加坚固。亲密的友谊会使人的生活丰富多彩。确保友谊之花兴盛不败的诸要素是：诚实、质朴、体谅和某些共同的兴趣。

环境和人都处于不断变化和发展之中。

❼ gravitate
/ˈgrævɪteɪt/
vi. 受吸引
❽ candidly
/ˈkændɪdlɪ/
adv. 坦白而诚实地
❾ ridicule
/ˈrɪdɪkjuːl/
v. 嘲笑
❿ deride
/dɪˈraɪd/
vt. 嘲弄；嘲笑
⓫ solidify
/səˈlɪdɪfaɪ/
v. 变得坚固

Circumstances and people are constantly changing. Some friendships last "forever"; others do not. Nevertheless, friendship is an essential ingredient[12] in the making of a healthful, rewarding life.

有的友谊天长地久，有的昙花一现。然而，友谊的确是使人的一生健康且过得有意义所不可缺少的组成部分。

⑫ ingredient
/ɪnˈɡriːdɪənt/
n. 要素；组分

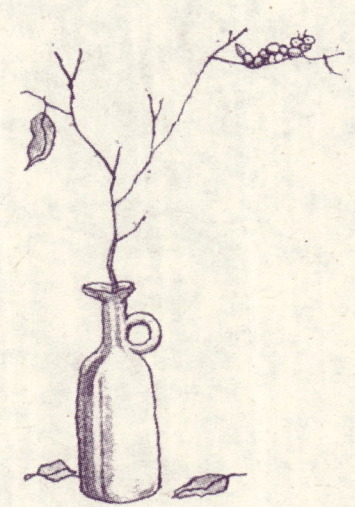

A simple turth about happiness
快乐真言

If you choose to find the positive in virtually every situation, you will be blessed.

如果你实际上在任何情况下都宁愿发现积极的方面，你准会因此而快乐。

I was not a particularly happy child, and like most teenagers, I reveled in¹ my angst². One day, however, it occurred to me that I was taking the easy way out. Anyone could be unhappy; it took no courage or effort. True challenge lay in struggling to be happy.

The notion that we have to work at happiness comes as news to many people. We assume it's a feeling that comes as a result of good things that just happen to us, things over which we have little or no control.

But the opposite is true: happiness is largely under our control. It is a battle to be waged and not a feeling to be awaited.

To achieve a happier life, it's necessary to overcome some stumbling blocks³, three of which are:

1. *Comparison with Others.*
Most of us compare ourselves with anyone we think is happier—a relative, an acquaintance or, often, someone we barely know. I once met a young man who struck me as particularly successful and happy. He spoke of his love for his beautiful wife and their daughters, and of his joy at being a radio talk-show host in a city he loved. I remember thinking he was one of those lucky few for whom everything goes effortlessly right.

Then we started talking about the Internet. He blessed its existence, he told me, because he could look up information on multiple sclerosis⁴ —the terrible disease afflicting⁵ his wife. I felt like a

小时候我并不特别快乐,和大多数十来岁的孩子一样,终日闷闷不乐。可是有一天,我茅塞顿开。任何人都可能不快乐,因为不快乐无需勇气,无需费力;然而真正的挑战在于努力使自己快乐。

我们必须为得到快乐作出努力,这种看法对很多人来说简直是闻所未闻。我们常以为快乐是因为我们碰上一些好事而产生的一种感觉,对于这些好事我们很少或者几乎无法控制。

然而,事实恰恰相反:快乐大都由我们自己控制,它不是袖手等来的一种感觉,而是准备发动的一场战斗。

要过上更加快乐的生活,必须清除一些绊脚石,其中三个绊脚石是:

1. 和别人比较

我们多数人总是把自己同我们认为比自己快乐的人进行比较——例如:一个亲戚,一个熟人,甚至常常是一个我们不太了解的人。我曾经遇到一个年轻人,在我看来,他非常成功而且快乐。他谈到了对美丽的妻子和女儿们的爱,谈到了对在自己喜欢的城市里做一个电台脱口秀节目主持人的欢欣。记得当时我以为他属于那种特别幸运的人,对他们而言,所有的事情都一帆风顺,做起来

❶ **revel in**
深爱,酷爱;沉迷于
❷ **angst**
/æŋst/
n. 烦恼,焦虑不安
❸ **stumbling block**
绊脚石
❹ **sclerosis**
/sklɪˈrəʊsɪs/
n. 硬化症
❺ **afflict**
/əˈflɪkt/
vt. 折磨,使痛苦

fool for assuming nothing unhappy existed in his life.

2. Images of Perfection.

Almost any of us have images of how life should be. The problem, of course, is that only rarely do people's jobs, spouses and children live up to[6] these imagined ideals.

Here's a personal example: No one in my family had ever divorced. I assumed that marriage was for life. So when my wife and I divorced three years after the birth of our son, my world caved in[7]. I was a failure in my own eyes.

I later remarried but confided to[8] my wife, Fran that I couldn't shake the feeling that my family life had failed. She asked me what was wrong with our family now (which included her daughter from a previous marriage and my son). I had to admit that, aside from the pain of being with my son only half the time (my ex-wife and I shared custody), our family life was wonderful.

"Then why don't you celebrate it?" she asked.

That's what I decided to do. But first I had to get rid of the image of a "perfect" family.

3. "Missing Tile" Syndrome.

One effective way of sabotaging[9] happiness is to look at something and be fixated on[10] even the smallest flaw. It's like looking up at a filed ceiling and concentrating on the space where one

不费吹灰之力。

后来我们开始谈论因特网。他告诉我，他感谢因特网的存在，因为他能够从网上查询关于多发性硬化症的信息——这种可怕的疾病一直折磨着他的妻子。我觉得自己很愚蠢，竟会认为他生活中没有任何不快乐的事情。

2. 幻想完美

几乎我们每个人都有自己的想象，想象生活该是什么样子。可是，问题显而易见，人们的工作、配偶和孩子很少达到想象中的理想境界。

我就有这样的经历：以前我们家从来没有人离过婚。我也认为婚姻应该是白头到老的。因此，在儿子出生三年后我和妻子离婚时，我的世界也随之塌陷。在我看来，我是个失败者。

后来我再婚了。我向妻子弗兰坦露心事，我不能摆脱家庭生活已经失败的感觉。她问我现在的家庭(包括她同前夫生的女儿，还有我自己的儿子)有什么不好。我不得不承认，除了我和前妻对儿子有共同的监护权(即我和前妻分担监护之责)使我和儿子相处的时间只有一半——这让我感到痛苦之外，我们的家庭生活是非常美好的。

❻ **live up to**
达到(符合)…的标准

❼ **cave in**
倒塌；塌陷

❽ **confide to**
交代；吐露(秘密)

❾ **sabotage**
/'sæbətɑːʒ/
vt. 破坏；捣乱

❿ **fixated on**
专注的，集中于某一事物的

tile is missing. As a bald man told me, "Whenever I enter a room, all I see is hair."

Once you've determined what your missing tile[11] is, explore whether acquiring it will really make you happy. Then do one of three things: get it, replace it with a different tile, or forget about it and focus on the tiles in your life that are not missing.

I've spent years studying happiness, and one of the most significant conclusions I've drawn is this: there is little correlation[12] between the circumstances of people's lives and how happy they are. A moment's reflection should make this obvious. We all know people who have had a relatively easy life yet are essentially unhappy. And we know people who have suffered a great deal but generally remain happy.

The first secret is gratitude[13]. All happy people are grateful. Ungrateful people cannot be happy. We tend to think that being unhappy leads people to complain, but it's truer to say that complaining leads to people becoming unhappy.

The second secret is realizing that happiness is a by-product[14] of something else. The most obvious sources are those pursuits that give our lives purpose—anything from studying insects to playing baseball. The more passions we have, the more happiness we're likely to experience.

Finally, the belief that something permanent transcends[15] us

她问我:"既然如此,你为什么不庆贺一番呢?"

这正是我决定去做的。但是首先,我必须去除心中对"完美"家庭的印象。

3. "缺砖"综合症

有一个方法破坏快乐很奏效,那就是看待事物时紧盯住哪怕是最小的瑕疵。这就好比向上看那瓷砖拼成的天花板,眼睛只注意缺少了一块瓷砖的那个地方。正如一个秃顶的人告诉我的:"我无论何时走进一个房间,看到的都是头发。"

一旦你确定了缺少的那块瓷砖是什么,就要琢磨一下,有了它是否会真正给你带来快乐。然后在下面三种办法中任选其一:找到它;用另一块瓷砖替换它;或者干脆忘掉它,把注意力集中在你生活中没有缺失的瓷砖上。

我研究快乐多年,得出的一个最重要的结论是:人们的生活情况和快乐程度没有多少关联。我们只需思考片刻就可以看出这个结论是显然成立的。我们都认识这么一些人,他们生活比较安逸却根本不快乐;我们也知道有些人虽然遭受巨大的痛苦却通常仍然快乐。

秘密之一在于感激。所有快乐的人都怀

⑪ tile
/taɪl/
n. 瓷砖
⑫ correlation
/ˌkɒrəˈleɪʃn/
n. 相互的关系
⑬ gratitude
/ˈɡrætɪtjuːd/
n. 感激
⑭ by-product
/ˈbaɪprɒdʌkt/
n. 副产品
⑮ transcend
/trænˈsend/
vt. 超越

and that our existence has some larger meaning can help us be happier. We need a spiritual or religious faith, or a philosophy of life.

Your philosophy should encompass[16] this truism[17]: if you choose to find the positive in virtually every situation, you will be blessed, and if you choose to find the awful, you will be cursed[18]. As with happiness itself, this is largely your decision to make.

有感激之情，不念恩情的人不可能快乐。我们常常以为人们因为不快乐才发牢骚，但是更为准确的说法是，牢骚满腹才使人们变得不快乐。

　　秘密之二在于认识到快乐是一种副产品。快乐最明显的一些来源是能赋予我们生活意义的那些追求——任何事，从研究昆虫到打棒球。我们拥有的激情越多，可能体验到的快乐也会越多。

　　最后，相信某种永恒的东西超越我们，相信我们的存在具有某种更宏大的意义——这会有助于我们感到更加快乐。我们需要一种精神信仰或宗教信仰，或者一种人生哲学。

　　你的哲学应该包含这个不言而喻的道理：如果你实际上在任何情况下都宁愿发现积极的方面，你准会因此而快乐；如果你宁愿发现糟糕的方面，你将会因此而痛苦。至于快乐本身，这主要看你自己如何决定了。

⑯ encompass
/ɪnˈkʌmpəs/
vt. 包含，包括

⑰ truism
/ˈtruːɪzəm/
n. 自明之理

⑱ curse
/kɜːs/
v. 为…所苦

To be a better friend
做个更好的朋友

A friendship network is absolutely crucial for our well-being as adults.

友谊的圈子对我们成年人的幸福至关重要。

Back when we were kids, the hours spent with friends were too numerous to count. There were marathon telephone conversations, all-night studying and giggling sessions. Even after boyfriends entered the picture, our best friends remained irreplaceable. And time was the means by which we nurtured those friendships. Now as adult women we never seem to have enough time for anything. Husbands, kids, careers and avocations[1]— all require attention; too often, making time for our friends comes last on the list of priorities. And yet, ironically, we need our friends as much as ever in adulthood. A friendship network is absolutely crucial for our well-being[2] as adults. We have to do the hard work of building and sustaining the network. Here are some important ways for accomplishing this.

Let go of your less central friendships. Many of our friendships were never meant to last a lifetime. It's natural that some friendships have time limits. Furthermore, now everyone has a busy social calendar, so pull back from some people that you don't really want to draw close to and give the most promising friendship a fair chance to grow.

Be willing to "drop everything" when you're truly needed. You may get a call from a friend who is really depressed over a certain problem when you are just sitting down to enjoy a romantic dinner with your husband. This is just one of those instances when a friend's needs mattered more. Sometimes, because of our unbreakable commitments or other circumstances, we simply can't give a needy friend the time we'd like. If you can't be there

① **avocation**
/ˌævəˈkeɪʃən/
n. 业余爱好

② **well-being**
n. 幸福，健康

在孩提时代，我们和朋友呆在一起的时间不计其数：马拉松式的电话交谈，整夜在一起学习和玩耍。即使在交了男朋友之后，我们最好的朋友的位置还是不可取代。正是在一起的时间培养了我们之间的友谊。现在我们都是成年女子了，时间似乎总不够用。丈夫、孩子、事业和业余爱好都要投入精力，因而很多时候便把朋友放到了最后。然而出人意料的是，我们在成年时代和儿童时代一样需要朋友。友谊的圈子对我们成年人的幸福至关重要。我们必须努力去建立和保持这个圈子。以下便是达到这个目的的几个重要方法。

舍得放弃无足轻重的友情。许多友情本来就不能终生维持。有的友情随时光的流逝而消失是情理之中的事。此外，现在每个人都有很多的社会应酬，所以，放弃那些你并不真正想接近的人，以便有更多的时间去培养那些最重要的友情。

急朋友之所急。当你刚刚坐下想和丈夫享受一顿浪漫的晚餐时，你的朋友却突然打来电话，她正为某一问题感到沮丧。有些情况下，朋友之需显得更为重要，这就是其中的一个例子。有时候，因为我们另有承诺，不能食言或有其他特殊情况，我们虽然想助

at that given moment, say something like, "I wish I could be with you — I can hear that you're in pain. May I call you tomorrow?" Be sure your friend knows she is cared about.

Take advantage of the mails. Nearly all of us have pals living far away — friends we miss very much. Given the limited time available for visits and the high price of phone calls, writing is a fine way to keep in touch — and makes both sender and receiver feel good. Besides, letters, cards and postcards have the virtue of being tangible[3] — friends can keep them and reread them for years to come.

Risk expressing negative feelings. When time together is tough to come by, it's natural to want the mood during that time to be upbeat[4]. And many people fear that others will think less of you if you express the negative feelings like anger and hurt. Remember honesty is the key to keeping a friendship real. Sharing your pain will actually deepen a friendship.

Don't make your friends' problems your own. Sharing your friend's grief is the way you show deep friendship. But taking on your friend's pain doesn't make that pain go away. There's a big difference between empathy[5] or recognizing a friend's pain, and over identification, which makes the sufferer feel even weaker. Remember troubled people just need their friends to stay grounded in their own feelings.

Never underestimate the value of loyalty. Loyalty has always

一臂之力，但苦于没有时间。如果你不能及时给朋友以帮助，那么不妨对她说，"我真希望能陪陪你——我能听出来你很痛苦。我明天给你打电话行吗？"一定要让你的朋友知道你对她的关心。

利用鸿雁传书。几乎我们所有人都有远在异地让我们非常想念的朋友。如果抽不出时间去探访，电话费又那么贵，那么写信是保持联系的好方法。这种方式让写信人和收信人都感到很高兴。而且，信件、卡片和明信片的优点是看得见摸得着，朋友可以将其保存，以后还可以再读。

坦露心中的抑郁。大家聚在一起不容易，自然希望彼此都有个好心情。好多人都担心，把自己的消极情绪——愤怒和伤心等吐露出来会让人家瞧不起。记住以诚相待是保持友谊真实的关键。让朋友分担你的痛苦其实反倒会加深友谊。

感受朋友的痛苦要恰如其分。分担朋友的痛苦是表露友情的一种方式。但是承受朋友的痛苦并不能消除其痛苦。心灵相通即理解朋友的痛苦与过分感受朋友的痛苦有很大区别。过分感受这种痛苦会使处在痛苦中的朋友更加脆弱。记住，处于逆境中的人需要的只是朋友的理解和支持。

❸ tangible
/ˈtændʒəbl/
adj. 可触摸的，有形的

❹ upbeat
/ˈʌpbiːt/
adj. 欢乐的，愉快的

❺ empathy
/ˈempəθɪ/
n. 同感，共感

been rated as one of the most desired qualities in friends. True loyalty can be a fairly subtle[6] thing. Some people feel it means that, no matter what, your friend will always take your side. But real loyalty is being accepting the person, not necessarily of certain actions your friend might take.

Give the gift of time as often as time allows. Time is what we don't have nearly enough of — and yet, armed with a little ingenuity[7], we can make it to give it to our friends. The trick is remembering that a little is better than none and that you can do two things at once. For instance, if you both go for a weekly aerobics[8], go on the same day. If you both want to go on vacation, schedule the same destination[9].

切勿低估忠诚的价值。忠诚一直被列为朋友间最重要的品质之一。真正的忠诚是件相当微妙的事情。有人认为忠诚意味着不管你做什么，你的朋友总是站在你这边。但真正的忠诚指的是接受其人，而不一定赞同其所有的行为。

巧妙利用时间，增进友谊。时间似乎总是不够用，但稍微变通一下便可以为朋友挤出时间来。重要的是要记住时间即使少一点也总比没有好，而且有时你可以一箭双雕。比如说，如果你和某位朋友每个星期都要去做一次健美操，那么就安排同一天去。如果双方都要去度假，那么不妨选择同一个去处。

❻ **subtle**
/ˈsʌtl/
n.难以察觉或描述的

❼ **ingenuity**
/ˌɪndʒəˈnjuːɪti/
n. 机灵，创造性

❽ **aerobics**
/eəˈrəʊbɪks/
n.健美操

❾ **destination**
/ˌdestɪˈneɪʃn/
n.目的地

Every day is a gift from God
每一天都是上帝赐予的礼物

Don't ever save anything for a special occasion.
Every day you're alive is a special occasion.

不要再攒着什么东西等什么特别的场合了。活着的每一天没有哪天不是特别的。

My brother-in-law opened the bottom drawer of my sister's bureau and lifted out a tissue-wrapped package. "This," he said, "is not a slip[1]. This is lingerie[2]," He discarded the tissue and handed me the slip. It was exquisite; silk, handmade and trimmed with a cobweb[3] of lace. The price tag with an astronomical figure on it was still attached. "Jan bought this the first time we went to New York, at least 8 or 9 years ago. She never wore it. She was saving it for a special occasion. Well, I guess this is the occasion." He took the slip from me and put it on the bed with the other clothes we were taking to the mortician[4]. His hands lingered on the soft material for a moment, then he slammed the drawer shut and turned to me, "Don't ever save anything for a special occasion. Every day you're alive is a special occasion."

I remembered those words through the funeral and the days that followed when I helped him and my niece attend to all the sad chores that follow an unexpected death. I thought about them on the plane returning to California from the Midwestern town where my sister's family lives. I thought about all the things that she hadn't seen or heard or done. I thought about the things that she had done without realizing that they were special. I'm still thinking about his words, and they've changed my life.

I'm reading more and dusting[5] less. I'm sitting on the deck and admiring the view without fussing about the weeds in the garden. I'm spending more time with my family and friends and less time in committed meetings. Whenever possible, life should be a pattern of experience to savor[6], not endure. I'm trying to recognize

姐夫打开姐姐的书桌最下面的抽屉，拿出一包用纸裹着的东西。"这个"，他说，"不再是什么衬裙，是睡裙了。"他扔了裹在外面的纸，将那件衬裙递给我。那是一件做工精美的衣服，真丝质料，手工制造，还有轻盈透明的花边。标着天文数字的价目标签依然系在上面。"我们第一次去纽约时，詹就把它买了下来。少说也有8、9年了，她没舍得穿，说要等到特别的场合再穿。唉！我想现在是时候了！"他从我手中拿回衬裙，把它和床上那些我们准备送到殡仪员那里的衣服放在一起。他的手在那柔软的面料上停留了好一阵子，尔后"砰"地关上抽屉，转身对我说："不要再攒着什么东西等什么特别的场合了。活着的每一天没有哪天不是特别的。"

在整个葬礼及后来帮助他和外甥女打理这场突如其来的变故后一切令人伤心的琐事期间，我的耳际一直回响着那番话。在从姐姐家住的中西部城市返回加州的飞机上，我又想起那番话。我想到了那些姐姐从未遇见过的、听到过的或尝试过的种种事情；想到了那些她虽做了但并没有意识到有多么特别的事情。时至今日，我依旧想着那番话，它改变了我的一生。

❶ **slip**
/slɪp/
n. 衬裙，女内衣

❷ **lingerie**
/ˈlænʒəriː/
n. 睡裙，女内衣

❸ **cobweb**
/ˈkɒbweb/
n. 蜘蛛网状的东西

❹ **mortician**
/mɔːˈtɪʃn/
n. 殡仪业者

❺ **dust**
/dʌst/
vt. 除尘

❻ **savor**
/ˈseɪvə/
vt. 品尝，欣赏

these moments now and cherish them.

I'm not "saving" anything; we use our good china and crystal for every special event—such as losing a pound, getting the sink unstopped, the first camellia[7] blossom. I wear my good blazer[8] to the market if I feel like it. I'm not saving my good perfume for special parties; clerks in hardware stores and tellers in banks have noses that function as well as my party-going friends. "Someday" and "one of those days" are losing their grip[9] on my vocabulary. If it's worth seeing or hearing or doing, I want to see and hear and do it now.

I'm not sure what my sister would have done had she known that she wouldn't be here for the tomorrow we all take for granted. I think she would have called family members and a few close friends. She might have called a few former friends to apologize and mend fences for past squabbles[10]. I like to think she would have gone out for a Chinese dinner, her favorite food. I'm guessing— I'll never know.

It's those little things left undone that would make me angry if I knew that my hours were limited. Angry because I put off seeing good friends whom I was going to get in touch with—someday. Angry because I hadn't written certain letters that I intended to write — one of those days. Angry and sorry that I didn't tell my husband and daughter often enough how much I truly love them. I'm trying very hard not to put off, hold back[11], or save anything that would add laughter and luster[12] to our lives. And every

我现在把时间花在读书上而不是打扫上。我会坐在露台上欣赏风景，而不再去担心是否该收拾园中的杂草。我花更多的时间和家人、朋友呆在一起，而不再去顾及那些例行的文山会海。不管什么时候，只要可能的话，生活都应该去品味享受，而非负累忍受。如今，我努力抓住这些时刻，并珍视它们。

我不再"攒"什么东西。在每一个特别的场合：譬如体重减了一磅、水槽疏通了、第一朵山茶花开时，我们都会用最好的瓷器和水晶器皿。如果我高兴的话，我就穿上漂亮的运动服去市场。我不再省下最好的香水等待特别的聚会，五金店的职员，银行里的出纳同聚会的朋友一样有能闻到香水的鼻子。"某一天"和"总有一天"在我的词汇表都失去了它们的吸引力。只要是值得看的、值得听的、值得做的，我便会立即付诸行动。

我不知道，如果姐姐知道明天——那个人人都以为自己可以拥有的明天——她将不在人世，她会做些什么。我想她会给家人和一些好朋友打电话；她也许会给一些从前的朋友打电话，为那些鸡毛蒜皮的争吵道歉，以重修旧好。我想她该出去吃她最喜欢的中国菜。但这只是我的猜测——我永远也不得

❼ **camellia**
/kəˈmiːlɪə/
n. 山茶花

❽ **blazer**
/ˈbleɪzə/
n. 运动上衣

❾ **grip**
/ɡrɪp/
n. 吸引力

❿ **squabble**
/ˈskwɒbl/
n. 口角，无谓的争吵

⓫ **hold back**
阻挡,阻碍

⓬ **luster**
/ˈlʌstə/
n. 光亮，光彩

morning when I open my eyes, I tell myself that it is special. Every day, every minute, every breath truly is... a gift from God.

而知了。

假如我自知时日无多，使我懊恼的很可能就是那些尚未完成的小事。我会懊恼，因为我一再推迟拜访好友的时间，总想着改天再去联系；我会懊恼，因为我一直没写我要写的信——我想总有一天会写的。会让我懊恼和遗憾的是，我没有经常告诉丈夫和女儿我全心地深深地爱着他们。如今，我尽力不再推迟、阻碍或保留起能给我们的生活带来欢乐和热情的东西。每天清晨，当我睁开眼睛，我都会告诉自己"今天是个特别的日子"。每一天、每一分钟、每一次呼吸……真的都是上帝恩赐的礼物！

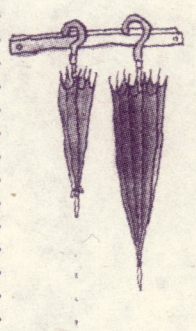

A dance with Dad
和父亲共舞

My father squeezes my hand and smiles at me. All the years that I refused to dance with him melt away now.

父亲紧攥着我的手向我微笑。多年来拒绝与他共舞的隔阂顷刻间烟消云散。

I am dancing with my father at my parents' 50th-wedding-annniversary celebration. The band is playing an old-fashioned waltz as we move gracefully across the floor. His hand on my waist is as guiding as it always was, and he hums the tune to himself in a steady, youthful way. Around and around we go, laughing and nodding to the other dancers.

We are the best dancers on the floor, they tell us. My father squeezes my hand and smiles at me. All the years that I refused to dance with him melt away[1] now. And those early times come back.

I remember when I was almost three and my father came home from work, swooped[2] me into his arms and began to dance me around the table. My mother laughed at us, told us dinner would get cold. But my father said, "She's just caught the rhythm of the dance! Our dinner can wait." Then he sang out, "Roll out the barrel, let's have a barrel of fun," and I sang back, "Let's get those blues[3] on the run."

We danced through the years. One night when I was 15, lost in some painful, adolescent mood. My father put on a stack of records and teased[4] me to dance with him. "C'mon," he said, "let's get those blues on the run."

When I turned away from him, my father put his hand on my shoulder, and I jumped out of the chair screaming, "Don't touch me! I am sick and tired of dancing with you!"

在我父母的金婚庆典上，我和父亲共舞。乐队奏着古老的华尔兹，我们在舞池中随着音乐优雅地翩翩起舞。他一如既往地将手放在我的腰际引领着舞步，嘴里和年轻人一样从容地哼着乐曲。我们跳了一圈又一圈，不时笑着向其他舞者点头致意。

人们称赞我们是场内跳得最好的一对。父亲紧攥着我的手向我微笑。多年来拒绝与他共舞的隔阂顷刻间烟消云散。往昔的美好时光重又回来。

我记得在我快3岁的时候，他下班回家猛地把我抱在怀里围着餐桌跳起舞来。妈妈看得直笑，说晚饭都要凉了。可父亲说："她刚跟上舞蹈的节奏！晚饭可以等会儿吃。"接着他就唱了起来："把桶滚出来，我们的滚桶多好玩，"我也唱着回应："带走忧郁与烦恼。"

我们这样跳了很多年。在我15岁那年的一个晚上，我正沉溺于少女的莫名烦恼中，父亲放上一摞唱片强拉我和他跳舞。他说："跳吧，带走忧郁与烦恼。"

我背过脸不理他，父亲又将手放到我的肩上。我一下子从椅子上蹦起来冲着他尖叫："别碰我！我讨厌和你跳舞！"

从他脸上可以看出他受到了伤害，可是

❶ melt away
消失，融化
❷ swoop
/swu:p/
vi. 突然袭击
❸ blue
/blu:/
adj. 沮丧，忧郁
❹ tease
/ti:z/
vt. 哄；强求

I saw the hurt on his face, but words were out and I could not call them back. I ran to my room sobbing[5] hysterically[6].

We did not dance together after that night. I found other partners, and my father waited up for me after dances, sitting in his favorite chair. Sometimes he would be asleep when I came in, and I would wake him, saying, "If you were so tired, you should have gone to bed."

"No, no," he'd say. "I was just waiting for you."

Then we'd lock up the house and go to bed.

My father waited up for me through my high-school and college years when I danced my way out of his life.

Shortly after my first child was born; my mother called to tell me my father was ill. "A heart problem," she said. "now, don't come. It's three hundred miles. It would upset your father."

A proper diet restored[7] him to good health. My mother wrote that they had joined a dance club. "The doctor says it's a good exercise. You remember how your father loves to dance."

Yes, I remembered. My eyes filled up with remembering.

When my father retired, we mended[8] our way back together

我话已出口无法收回。我跑回自己房中放声大哭。

从那晚后，我们再也没有一起跳过舞。我有了别的舞伴，而父亲总是坐在他最喜爱的椅子上熬夜等我舞罢归来。有时，我回到家时他已经睡着，我便叫醒他说："你要是这么累，就该上床去睡觉。"

而他总说："不，不，我等你呢。"

然后我们便锁上大门，各自上床睡觉。

整个中学和大学期间，当我出去跳舞时，他就这样熬夜等我。

我的第一个孩子出生后不久，妈妈打来电话说爸爸病了。她说："是心脏的问题。现在你不要来。咱们离着300英里地呢。你赶回来爸爸心里会不安的。"

合适的饮食调养使父亲恢复了健康。妈妈来信说他们参加了一个舞蹈俱乐部，"医生说这是一种很好的运动。你该记得他是多么的喜欢跳舞。"

我当然不会忘记。眼前闪过的尽是对当年的回忆。

父亲退休后，我们又一起努力修复了关系，每次见面都少不了拥抱和亲吻。他和孙辈跳舞，但从不找我跳。我知道他是在等我道歉，可我却怎么也找不到合适的字眼。

❺ **sob**
/sɒb/
v. 呜咽
❻ **hysterically**
/hɪˈstɪərɪklɪ/
adv. 歇斯底里地
❼ **restore**
/rɪˈstɔː/
v. 使恢复
❽ **mend**
/mend/
v. 改善

again; hugs and kisses were common when we visited each other. He danced with the grandchildren, but he did not ask me to dance. I knew he was waiting for an apology from me. I could never find the right words.

As my parents' 50th anniversary approached, my brothers and I met to plan the party. My older brother said, "Do you remember that night you wouldn't dance with him? Boy, was he mad? I couldn't believe he'd get so mad about a thing like that. I'll bet you haven't danced with him since."

I did not tell him he was right.

My younger brother promised to get the band. "Make sure they can play waltzes and polkas," I told him.

I did not tell him that all I wanted to do was dance once more with my father.

When the band began to play after dinner, my parents took the floor. They glided[9] around the room, inviting the others to join them. The guests rose to their feet, applauding the golden couple. My father danced with his granddaughters, and then the band began to play the "Beer Barrel Polka".

"Roll out the barrel," I heard my father singing. Then I knew it was time. I wound my way[10] through a few couples and tapped my daughter on the shoulder.

随着二老金婚纪念日的临近，我和兄弟们聚到一起安排庆典宴会。哥哥说："还记得那天晚上你不肯和他跳舞的事吗？好家伙，他是着了迷。真难相信他会对跳舞那么入迷。我敢说从那天以后你再也没和他跳过舞了。"

他说对了，但是我没有告诉他。

弟弟答应去找乐队。我对他说："一定要找能演奏华尔兹和波尔卡的。"

我没有告诉他，我就希望能和父亲再跳一回舞。

晚餐过后，乐队开始演奏，我父母走进舞场，滑着舞步绕场邀请大家同乐。客人全都起立，用掌声向金婚的老两口祝福。父亲轮流和孙女们跳舞，这时乐队开始奏起了"啤酒桶波尔卡"。

我听到老爸在唱"把桶滚出来……"，知道是时候了。我绕过几对跳舞的人，拍了拍女儿的肩膀。我说："对不起，我想该轮到我跳了。"我直视着父亲的双眸，几乎把要说的话噎在了嗓子眼儿里。

爸爸站在那儿，一动不动。我们四目对视，时光仿佛又回到了我15岁时的那个夜晚。我声音发颤地接着唱道："带走忧愁与烦恼。"

父亲弯身示意说："噢，对。我一直在等着

⑨ glide
/glaɪd/
vi. 滑动，滑行
⑩ wind one's way
绕行

"Excuse me," I said, looking directly into my father's eyes and almost choking[11] on my words, "but I believe this is my dance."

My father stood rooted[12] to the spot. Our eyes met and traveled back to that night when I was 15. In a trembling voice, I sang, "Let's get those blues on the run."

My father bowed and said, "Oh ,yes. I've been waiting for you."

Then he started to laugh, and we moved into each other's arms.

你呢。"

然后他开怀大笑,我们投进了彼此的怀抱。

⓫ choke
/tʃəuk/
v.哽咽

⓬ root
/ruːt/
v.使立定不动

A daughter thanks her mother
女儿对母亲的感谢

Your greatest gift to me was teaching me how to be a good mother to my own children.

您留给我最宝贵的礼物,就是教会了我如何为我自己的孩子做一个好妈妈。

Dear Mum,

    I haven't written many letters to you before, as we've almost always been able to just pick up the phone and have a chat[1], so it's hard to know how to start.

    Of course, all the usual things apply—we all miss you and hope you're all right wherever you are.

    When you left us, it took a little while for it to sink in that I would never see you again. I guess it was a bit like you being away on a trip or those times when we didn't find the time to even speak on the phone for a week or so.

    I realise now there are too many things left unsaid—as everyone always says—and too many questions unasked. Silly things really, like yesterday, when I was doing my washing, I wondered how you felt when you got your first automatic[2] washing machine. I can still remember the old machine you had when I was a child. Though, I guess I know the answers to most of the things about you.

    Dad is finding life difficult without you and his loneliness is almost unbearable[3] to me, as there's so little I can do to help him. I think in time he'll find some interests and make a new kind of life. But at the moment he seems only to look forward to the time when he can join you again.

    Emily and I are feeling a little better each day and, in a way,

亲爱的妈妈:

以前没有给您写过多少信,因为我们几乎总能拿起电话,聊上一聊,所以真不知道如何下笔。

当然,那些老套话都可以用——我们全都想念您,无论您现在身在何方,祝愿您万事如意。

在您离开我们的时候,我曾有一段时间陷入永远不能再见到您的沉思之中,我想那情形有点像您出门旅行了,或者就像我们有时一个星期左右都没时间通电话一样。

我现在意识到有太多的话还没有说(正如大家常说的那样),有太多的问题还没有问。其实尽是些愚蠢的问题,比如昨天,在我洗衣服的时候,我想知道您买来第一台自动洗衣机时有什么感觉。我还能记得我小时候您的那台旧洗衣机。然而,我想有关您的事情,我大都知道答案。

没有了您,爸爸觉得日子很难熬。他的孤独让我几乎无法忍受,因为我帮不了他多少忙。我想早晚他会找到些感兴趣的事,开始一种新的生活。但是眼下他似乎只盼望与你再次相聚。

我和埃米莉的感觉日渐好转。从某种意义上来讲,您的过世使我们的关系更加密切

❶ chat
/tʃæt/
n. 聊天;闲谈
❷ automatic
/ˌɔːtə'mætɪk/
adj. 自动的
❸ unbearable
/ʌn'beərəbl/
adj. 难以忍受的

your going has brought us closer together. We seem to understand each other better at the moment and maybe eventually we'll have the sort of relationship that really close sisters enjoy.

We've both found strengths in each other over the past weeks, and these are a huge comfort. Perhaps we never needed to look for them before, because we had you to be strong for us.

I guess I'm lucky to have my own children to keep me so busy. I don't have much time to <u>dwell on</u>[4] my sadness but sometimes I crave[5] the peace to just have a private think about you.

For a couple of weeks after you died, my brain seemed to go crazy, searching through its memory banks for something I could keep in my heart which was special to you and me. One day it came to me—the tour we made of some special garden.

Remember the day it poured with rain the whole time but we were determined to make the most of it? I enjoyed just being with you by myself, without the children clamouring[6] for your attention. The gardens were beautiful despite the rain and you bought me a rose I'd admired for my own garden.

For a while after your death, I expected to feel your presence around me as Dad and Emily seem to do with such ease. When I was out walking, I would look at the sky and wonder whether you could see me, or whether you were with me. At night I wondered whether you'd become a star, as some people believe.

了。此时此刻，我们似乎对彼此更加了解，也许最终我们会享有真正的姐妹们享有的那种亲密关系。

在过去的几周里，我们从彼此的身上找到了力量，这真是莫大的安慰。也许我们以前从不需要寻求这种力量，因为有您作我们的坚强后盾。

我想幸运的是我自己有了孩子，使我忙忙碌碌，因此没有多少时间老是沉湎在悲伤之中，但有时我渴望有安静的一刻，可以私下里去思念您。

在您去世后好几周里，我的大脑好像发了疯一样，拼命在我脑子的记忆库中寻找珍藏在我心底的某件事情——某件对你我二人都具有特殊意义的事情。有一天我终于想起来了——我们到一个特别的花园所作的那次旅行。

您还记得吗？那天一直下着倾盆大雨，但是我们打定主意，要充分利用这次机会好好玩一玩。我很高兴能单独和您在一起，没有孩子们的吵闹使您分神。尽管下着雨，花园还是很美。您给我买了一枝玫瑰，我一直希望自己的花园种有这种玫瑰。

您去世后的一段时间里，我期望能感到您就在我的身边，爸爸和埃米莉似乎毫不费

❹ **dwell on**
细想；评述
❺ **crave**
/kreɪv/
v.渴望
❻ **clamour**
/ˈklæmə/
vi.吵闹；叫喊

But as time passes, I think I'm closer to finding the truth. You're with me every time I comfort one of the children or try to find the right words to gently chastise[7] them. I listen for your words of wisdom and they come from within me because your greatest gift to me was teaching me how to be a good mother to my own children.

And although you're no longer here with us, I know in times of sadness or pain the children feel your arms around them just as I sense that I feel your arms around me, too. In years to come I hope your gift to me will be passed to my own children's children. And I know it's your voice telling me in these changing times the best thing we can give our children is love, because love is eternal[8] and love doesn't die. So long for now, and thank you from all of us.

Happy Mother's Day, Mum.

Love Carol

力地就能感到您的存在。在外边散步的时候，我常常仰望天空，想知道您是否能看见我，或者您是否和我在一起。在夜晚，我会想，您是否像有些人相信的那样变成了一颗星星。

但是随着时间的流逝，我想我差不多找到了真实的感觉。每当我安慰一个孩子的时候，或者要找出合适的语言来轻轻地责备他们的时候，您都同我在一起。如果我留神倾听您充满智慧的语言，它们就会从我的内心传来，因为您留给我最宝贵的礼物，就是教会了我如何为我自己的孩子做一个好妈妈。

虽然您已经不再同我们一起生活在这个世上，但我知道在痛苦和悲伤的时候，孩子们能感到您的臂膀拥抱着他们，就像我能感到您的臂膀也拥抱着我一样。在未来的岁月中，我希望把您留给我的礼物传给我的子孙。我知道那是您的声音在告诉我，在这个不断变化的时代，我们能留给我们孩子的最好的东西就是爱，因为爱是永恒的，爱是不朽的。后会有期，我们都衷心地感谢您。

祝您母亲节快乐，妈妈。

爱您的卡罗尔

❼ chastise
/tʃæˈstaɪz/
vt. (formal)责罚，惩罚

❽ eternal
/ɪˈtɜːnl/
adj. 永久的；永恒的

Books
书籍

No entertainment is so cheap as reading, nor any pleasure so lasting.

没有一种娱乐像读书那样便宜，也没有任何乐趣像读书那样持续久远。

Books are a guide in youth and an entertainment for age. They support us under solitude, and keep us from being a burden to ourselves.

— Jeremy Collier

The only true equalizers in the world are books; the only treasure-house open to all comers is a library.

—Dr. Langford

Perhaps no other thing has such power to lift the poor out of his poverty, the wretched[1] out of his misery, to make the burden-bearer forget his burden, the sick his suffering, the sorrower his grief, the downtrodden[2] his degradation, as books. They are friends to the lonely, companions to the deserted, joy to the joyless, hope to the hopeless, good cheer to the disheartened[3], a helper to the helpless. They bring light into darkness, and sunshine into shadow.

We may be poor, socially ostracized[4], shut out from all personal association with the great and the good, and yet be in the best society in the world, in books. We may live in palaces, converse with princes, be familiar with royalty, and associate with the greatest and noblest of all time.

The trend of many a life for good or ill, for success or failure, has been determined by a single book. The books which we read early in life are those which influence us most.

书籍是青年人的指南,老年人的娱乐。孤寂时,书籍给我们力量,使我们摆脱精神负担。

——杰里米·柯里尔

举世惟一真正平等待人者是书籍;对来者都开放的惟一宝库是图书馆。

——兰格弗博士

世上或许没有别的东西像书籍那样有这种力量:使穷人摆脱贫困,使不幸者脱离悲惨的处境,使肩负重担者忘掉负担,使病人忘掉痛苦,使伤心人忘掉忧伤,使受压迫的人忘掉屈辱。书籍是孤独者的朋友,是被遗弃者的同伴,是郁郁寡欢者的乐趣,是绝望者的希望,是沮丧者的兴奋剂,是无依无靠者的援助之手。书籍把光明带进黑暗,让阳光照射到阴暗的地方。

我们可能一文不名,遭到社会的摈弃,同大人物和善良人士没有来往,然而在书中,我们却可置身于世界上最理想的社会之中。我们可以居住在宫殿内,与王子晤谈,同王室成员熟识,总是和最伟大、最高尚的人士交往。

很多人的一生是好还是坏,是成功还是

❶ **wretched**
/ˈretʃɪd/
 adj. 不幸的,可怜的

❷ **downtrodden**
/ˈdaʊnˌtrɒdn/
adj. 受压迫的

❸ **disheartened**
/dɪsˈhɑːtnd/
adj. 气馁的;沮丧的

❹ **ostracized**
/ˈɒstrəsaɪzd/
adj. 遭摈弃的

We form many of our opinions from our favorite books. The author whom we prefer is our most potent[5] teacher; we look at the world through his eyes. If we habitually read books that are elevating[6] in tone, pure in style, sound in reasoning, and keen in insight, our minds develop the same characteristics. If, on the contrary, we read weak or vicious[7] books, our minds contract the faults and vices of the books. We cannot escape the influence of what we read any more than we can escape the influence of the air that we breathe.

The best books are those which stir us up most and make us the most determined to do something and be something ourselves. The best books are those which lift us to a higher plane where we breathe a purer atmosphere. As we should associate with people who can inspire us to nobler deeds, so we should only read those books which have an uplifting power, and which stir us to make the most of ourselves and our opportunities.

Emerson had three rules for reading: never read a book that is not a year old; never read any but famous books; never read a book you do not like.

Libraries are no longer a luxury, but a necessity. A home without books and periodicals[8] and newspapers is like a house without windows. Children learn to read by being in the midst of books; they unconsciously absorb knowledge by handling them. No family can now afford to be without good reading.

失败的趋向都是由一本书决定的。幼年读过的书对我们影响最大。

我们的许多看法大都是从最喜欢的书中形成的。我们喜爱的作家是对我们最有影响力的老师；我们借助他的眼力观察世界。如果我们经常读的书语气是激励人心的，文体是洗练的，推理是正确的，洞察力是敏锐的，我们的心智就会发展成同样的特性。反之，如果阅读不健康的书籍，我们的心智就会沾染书里的缺点和邪恶。正如不能避免呼吸的空气的影响一样，我们不能避免所读书籍的影响。

最好的书最能激励我们，鞭策我们下最大决心做事，成为不同寻常的人。最好的书使我们达到更高水平，呼吸更为清新的空气。正如应该与鼓舞我们从事更崇高事业的人交往一样，应该只读那些有鼓舞力量、促使我们充分利用自己和机会的书籍。

爱默生读书有三条规则：绝不读问世不到一年的书；绝不读不著名的书；绝不读自己不喜爱的书。

"藏书不再是一种奢华，而是一种需要。没有书籍、期刊和报纸的家庭，就像一间没有窗户的居室。儿童们学会读书全靠优游于群书之中；经常翻阅书籍，孩子们会不知不觉地汲取知识。现如今，任何一个家庭都绝

❺ **potent**
/ˈpəʊtənt/
adj. (formal)有影响的；强有力的

❻ **elevating**
/ˈelɪveɪtɪŋ/
adj. 引人向上的

❼ **vicious**
/ˈvɪʃəs/
adj. 道德败坏的；堕落的

❽ **periodical**
/ˌpɪərɪˈɒdɪkl/
n. 期刊

Furnish your house with books rather than unnecessary furniture, or even pictures if you cannot afford all. Wear threadbare[9] clothes and patched[10] shoes if necessary, but do not pinch or economize on books. If you cannot give your children an academic education you can place within their reach a few good books which will lift them above their surroundings, into respectability and honour.

"No entertainment is so cheap as reading," says Mary Wortley Montagu; "nor any pleasure so lasting." Good books elevate the character, purify the taste, take the attractiveness out of low pleasures, and lift us upon a higher plane of thinking and living. It is not easy to be mean directly after reading a noble and inspiring book. The conversation of a man who reads for improvement or pleasure will be flavored by his reading; but it will not be about his reading.

Whatever you read, read with enthusiasm, with energy, read with the whole mind, if you would increase your mental stature, learn to absorb the mental and the moral life of a book, and assimilate[11] it into your life. He is the best reader who consumes the most knowledge and converts it into character. Mechanical readers remember words, the husks[12] of things, but digest nothing. They cram[13] their brains but starve their minds. If you are getting the most out of a book, you will feel a capacity for doing things which you never felt before.

对不能缺少良好的读物。

要是你无力购买所有的家具,就用书籍来装饰你的居室,不要没有必要的家具、甚至字画。如果必要的话,宁肯穿破衣烂鞋,也不要在买书上抠门吝啬。要是不能让儿女受到正规的学校教育,你可以把一些好书置于他们身旁,那些书会使他们跨越环境的藩篱,达到享有尊敬和荣誉的境界。

"没有一种娱乐像读书那样便宜,也没有任何乐趣像读书那样持续久远,"玛丽·沃特利·蒙塔古说。好书提高读者的品格,使趣味高雅,摆脱低级娱乐的引诱,使我们的思想和生活达到更高的水平。读过一本卓越的、鼓舞人心的书,就不容易马上心地卑鄙。为了进步或乐趣而读书的人,读书会给他的谈吐增添风趣;但谈话的内容并不涉及他所读的书。

如果你想提高精神境界,不论你读什么,你都要饱含热情、精力充沛、一心一意地读下去。学习吸收一本书的精神和道德的活力,融化到你的生活之中。最会读书的人能吞噬最多的知识并转化为自己的品质。死读书的人只记得字面词义和皮毛,但食而不化。他们只知填塞头脑,却智力贫乏。如果你从一本书中正在获得最大的收益,你就会感觉到一种你以前从未感觉到的做事能力。

❾ **threadbare**
/ˈθredbeə/
adj. 穿旧的;磨得很薄的
❿ **patched**
/ˈpætʃt/
adj. 打补丁的
⓫ **assimilate**
/əˈsɪmɪleɪt/
v. 吸收
⓬ **husk**
/hʌsk/
n. 外壳,空壳
⓭ **cram**
/kræm/
v. 尽力塞入

Tips for staying calm
保持平静的秘诀

If you're almost always irritable and abrupt, you may well feel that you're just too important to ever be kept waiting for anyone or anything.

如果你几乎总是急躁不安,你也许是觉得自己太重要了,等待不了任何人或任何事。

I watched the old man's fumbling[1] fingers as he slowly counted out the coins, one by one. I was all but dancing with impatience in the checkout line and sighed with exasperation[2]. Hearing me, he smiled apologetically—a tiny smile of humiliation at being feeble and holding up the world's business.

Then I became contrite[3]. Putting myself in his shoes, I realized that someday they might pinch my feet. I too, could become dependent on the kindness of strangers. I patted his frayed[4] sleeves. "Take your time," I said. "There's no hurry."

It occurred to me how often I have acted impatiently—honking[5] my horn the instant the light changed, speaking sharply to someone slow to understand. Did it matter? It did. When you're impatient, you're apt to be rude. And such behavior is counterproductive, making people angry or stubborn or uncooperative.

I decided to try becoming more patient and to develop various approaches for calming myself in stressful situations. I can't claim that these techniques transformed me into a model of patience, but they have helped me eliminate some impatience from my life and control most of it.

Allow for a margin of error. A friend had passed the interviews for an important new job; all that remained was for the president of the company to meet his wife.

At six, my friend and his wife were in the tunnel on their way

我望着那位老人不灵巧的手指慢慢地一个一个地数着硬币。我站在结账队伍里不耐烦地动来动去,恼怒地叹了口气。听到我的叹气声,他满脸歉意地笑了——一种由于自己虚弱无力而耽搁社会事务,感到不好意思的勉强的笑容。

我感到后悔了。我设身处地想了想,意识到总有一天自己也会处于同样的境地,也会依赖陌生人的善意。我拍了拍他早已磨损的衣袖,说道,"慢慢来,不用急。"

我想到自己有多少次表现出不耐烦来——绿灯一亮就开始按喇叭,对反应慢的人尖刻地说话。这样做有坏处吗?是的。当你不耐烦时,你很容易表现得粗鲁。这样的行为会招致反效果,使得别人生气、固执或者不予合作。

我决定要变得有耐心些,想出了各种办法使自己在焦虑之中平静下来。我不敢说这些办法把我变成了一个有耐心的楷模,但确实帮助我消除了生活中的一些不耐烦的情绪,在大部分场合控制住了自己。

为差错留有余地。一位朋友通过了一份重要的新工作的面试;现在只需让公司总裁见一见他的妻子了。

6.点钟时,我的朋友和他的妻子进入通往纽约的隧道,赶赴7.点钟的约会。7.点钟,他

❶ **fumbling**
/ˈfʌmblɪŋ/
adj. 笨手笨脚的
❷ **exasperation**
/ɪɡˌzæspəˈreɪʃn/
n. 恼怒;恼火
❸ **contrite**
/ˈkɒntraɪt/
adj. 懊悔的,悔悟的
❹ **fray**
/freɪ/
v.(使)磨损
❺ **honk**
/hɒnk/
v. 按汽车喇叭

into New York for a seven o'clock appointment. At seven, they were still in the tunnel, stuck behind an overturned tractor-trailer. When they finally reached the president's hotel, he had gone, leaving no message. He would not accept an explanation the next day. "You should have planned for delays," he said.

Impatient people don't like to waste time, so they cut things too closely. They budge the exact number of minutes that a journey or task should take, not allowing for the possibility of delay or the unexpected. It is better to provide a margin for error. The more important your appointment is, the more time should be allotted[6]. When an appointment absolutely can't be missed, it pays to allow ridiculous amounts of time.

Put things in perspective. Not setting a coveted[7] job is calamitous[8], but the consequences of being held up are seldom that serious. They are not worth getting impatient.

I've learned to ask myself, "What's the worst that can happen?" If the answer is that I'll miss the opening credits of a movie or the start of a ball game, I calm down. Will I even remember next week that I was ten minutes late today? Putting matters in perspective should ease your impatience.

Think ahead. One evening as an acquaintance was leaving for a weekend trip, her car wouldn't start—and three friends were waiting to be picked up on a street corner. She had no way of getting word to them; they were cold and miserable and worried

们还被困在隧道里，道路被一辆翻倒了的拖车堵塞了。当他们终于赶到总裁所住的宾馆时，总裁已经走了，没有留任何话。第二天他也不愿接受任何解释。"你应该考虑到路上的耽搁的，"总裁说。

没有耐心的人不愿意浪费时间，因此他们把时间卡得过紧。他们精确地计算一次旅行或者一次任务要花多少时间，而不考虑到发生耽搁或意外事件的可能性。最好是为差错留出余地。你要赶赴的约会越重要，你就越应该多分配些时间。如果某个约会是绝不能错过的，那就值得为它花去多得让你感到荒谬的时间。

摆正各种事情的位置。没有得到梦寐以求的工作是不幸的，但因为被耽搁而造成的结果很少有那么严重，因而不值得为此烦躁不安。

我已经学会了问自己："可能发生的最坏的事情是什么？"如果回答是我将错过电影开头的演员表部分或者球赛的开场，我就会平静下来。到了下个星期我还会记得今天迟到了10分钟吗？摆正各种事情的位置能够让你放松下来。

事先考虑。一天晚上，我认识的一个人准备出发去周末旅行，但她的汽车发动不了

❻ **allot**
/əˈlɒt/
v. 分配，分拨给

❼ **coveted**
/ˈkʌvɪtɪd/
adj. 梦寐以求的

❽ **calamitous**
/kəˈlæmɪtəs/
adj. 灾难性的，悲惨的

when she arrived an hour late. Since hearing her predicament[9], I've always arranged to meet people where they or I can be reached in case of delay. It enables me to be far more patient when things go wrong.

Be prepared. Waiting in airports is one of the most trying features of modern life. I was watching torrential[10] rains streak[11] the windows at Raleigh-Durham International Airport one morning when a man came up, took a word game from his pocket and asked if I wanted to play. We played with pleasure for the four hours our plane was delayed. Near us, a man worked on his <u>laptop computer</u>[12]. One woman went through a stack of catalogues methodically, turning down the corners of the pages, filling out older blanks. The most impatient people— the ones who prowled[13] the waiting area and complained loudly—were those who had nothing to do but put coins in the vending machines.

I now assume I'll encounter a delay, so I always carry a paperback. A friend works crossword puzzles.

Live for the moment. A man I knew was always racing impatiently into the future. If we met for a drink after work, the first thing he talked about was where we'd go for dinner; at dinner, he rushed through dessert to get to a movie; at the movie, he was on his feet before the last frame faded. And in the car on the way home, he was making plans for the next day, next week, next year.

了——而三位朋友正在一条街的拐角处等待她开车来接。她没有办法和他们取得联系；一个小时后她才到，他们已经冻得发抖、可怜兮兮、心急如焚了。听了她的尴尬经历之后，我就总是安排在能够联系上的地方与别人见面，以防耽搁的发生。这样使得我在事情出错时能变得有耐心多了。

做好准备。在机场候机是现代生活中最折磨人的特色之一。一天早上，我在罗利—达勒姆国际机场里望着雨水沿玻璃窗奔流而下。这时走过来一个人，他从口袋里掏出一份猜字游戏，问我愿不愿意玩。在飞机延误的4个小时里，我们高兴地玩着。在我们附近，一个男子在用手提电脑工作。一位妇女有条理地浏览了一大叠目录，并折记了页脚，填写了订购单。最没有耐心的人们——那些在候机区里来回走动、大声抱怨的人——是那些无事可做、只会往自动售货机里投币的人。

我现在总是假设自己可能遇到一次耽搁，所以我总会带着一本平装书。一位朋友则玩填字游戏。

享受当前这一刻。我认识一个人，他总是迫不及待地做下一步的事情。比如我们工作之余相约一起喝点酒，他谈论的第一件事就是到哪里去吃饭；吃饭时，他匆匆忙忙地

❾ predicament
/prɪˈdɪkəmənt/
n. 困境，尴尬的处境

❿ torrential
/təˈrenʃl/
adj. 奔流的，急流的

⓫ streak
/striːk/
vt. 留以条痕

⓬ laptop computer
手提电脑

⓭ prowl
/praʊl/
vt. 徘徊

Never did he live in the here and now. Consequently, he couldn't enjoy life.

I've come to appreciate that life has its own timetable. It takes nine months to make a baby, 21 years to make an adult. It takes a long time to become a good violinist or downhill skier. It also takes time to become a success and even more time to become a success as a person.

Perhaps the last thing for controlling impatience is to examine your own contribution to it. Are you unwilling to grant children time to learn, or slow people time to accomplish a task? If impatience is only occasional, your annoyance will pass. But if you're almost always irritable and abrupt, you may well feel that you're just too important to ever be kept waiting for anyone or anything.

You're not, of course; none of us are. If we can accept that the world is ours to enjoy but not made for our convenience, we'll be better able to move through it equably[14], more patient with the ordinary vicissitudes[15] of life and a good companion to our fellow human beings—and to ourselves.

吞下甜点,急着去看电影;在看电影时,最后一幕还没有结束,他就已经起身离开了。在开车回家的路上,他已经在为第二天、下个星期、明年做计划了。

他从来没有生活在此时此地。结果,他享受不到生活。

我已经欣赏到,生活自有它的时间表。孕育一个孩子要9个月时间,长大成人则要21年。要用很长的时间才能成为一名优秀的小提琴手或一名优秀的滑雪运动员。取得成功也需要时间——取得人生的成功需要更多的时间。

也许控制住烦躁情绪的最后一招是检查一下这种情绪是否由自己引起。你是不是不情愿给予孩子们学习的时间,或者行动迟缓的人们完成一件事的时间?如果只是偶然的不耐烦,那么你的恼怒就会过去。但如果你几乎总是急躁不安,你也许是觉得自己太重要了,等待不了任何人或任何事。

你当然没有这么重要;我们谁也没有这么重要。如果我们能够接受这一点,即这个世界是供我们去体会的,而不是为我们提供方便的,我们就会过得更平和些,更耐心地对待生活中的变迁,成为别人的——也是自己的——更好的伴侣。

⑭ **equably**
/ˈekwəblɪ/
adv. 平静地;性情温和地

⑮ **vicissitude**
/vɪˈsɪsɪtjuːd/
n. 变迁,成败

The little words that work marriage magic
创造婚姻奇迹的小小字眼

I'm so glad you're in my life.

我真高兴我的生命里有你。

Using terms of endearment[1] like honey or sweetheart from time to time is a small but important way to keep a marriage loving. These terms make the other person feel loved and special. There are some other words that can help make your spouse feel special and aware of how much you love and appreciate him.

'*Thank You.*' We would never not thank a friend or co-worker for helping us out. But sometimes we forget to thank the person we love most: our spouse. All couples forget now and then to thank each other for all they do. But thanking each other is a good habit to fall into[2] because gratitude[3] is necessary for the growth of love. Knowing that their actions are appreciated makes a couple more giving toward each other, and the more you give to each other the more your love will grow.

'*Please.*' Please, like thank you, is easy to forget to say, but it too is very important in a relationship. Because it is another way of letting your partner know you don't take him for granted and that his time and effort count.

'*You are great.*' Do you know that this sentence can make him feel good about himself all day? Now that you know how nice it makes him feel to be complimented, you should try to do it as often as you can. As an added bonus[4], he will begin paying compliments[5] to you more often. This is not surprising since, experts say, compliments are a two-way street. So the more compliments you give, the more you get. Often couples will think nice things about each other but not verbalize[6] their thoughts because they're

时常使用亲密的称呼，如"宝贝"、"亲爱的"等是让婚姻充满爱恋的小小的但相当重要的办法。这些亲热的字眼能让对方感到被爱，感到特殊。另外还有一些字眼能让你的配偶感到自己的特殊性，感到你是多么爱他，多么欣赏他。

　　"谢谢你" 我们在朋友或同事帮忙后绝不会忘记表示感谢。但有时，我们却忘了感谢我们最爱的人：我们的配偶。夫妻常常会忘记感谢对方所做的事情。但彼此表示感谢是应养成的好习惯，因为感激之情是使爱情之树常青所不可或缺的。看到自己所做的一切被对方欣赏会使你更愿意给予对方；而夫妻之间相互给予越多，爱就会增长越多。

　　"请" "请"和"谢谢"一样，是很容易被忽略的，而这一字眼在夫妻关系中也是十分重要的。因为它也能让你的配偶知道你并不认为他替你办事是理所当然的；相反，他花的时间和精力你都心领了。

　　"你真好" 你知道这句话能让他一整天都感觉良好吗？既然知道让他感受赞赏是多么舒服，就尽可能地去赞赏他吧！另外一个好处是，他也会更加经常地赞赏你了。这不足为奇。正如专家们所说，赞赏是条双行道。所以你越赞赏你的配偶，你便越能得到他的

---

❶ **endearment**
/ɪnˈdɪəmənt/
n. 亲爱，亲密

❷ **fall into**
开始

❸ **gratitude**
/ˈɡrætɪtjuːd/
n. 感激；感谢

❹ **bonus**
/ˈbəʊnəs/
n. 意外的好处

❺ **compliment**
/ˈkɒmplɪmənt/
n. 赞美的表示

❻ **verbalize**
/ˈvɜːbəlaɪz/
v. 用言语表达（思想或感情）

just not in the habit of doing so. But when one of them starts, the other will pick up on the cue[7] and begin doing the same.

'*I love you.*' in a new way A small variation[8] such as ' I love you more each day' can make a big difference in how you feel about each other. When you say 'I love you' the exact same way over and over, your spouse may start to discount[9] it. On the other hand, a fresh phrase can help keep the relationship fresh. For instance, you can expressed your love for him by saying 'I'm so glad you're in my life.' I'm sure he will be really impressed and touched, and you two will feel closer.

赞赏。通常夫妻彼此心里都有好感，但因为没有养成习惯，很少说出来，但是一旦其中一方开了口，另一方也会领会用意跟着做。

"我爱你"的新表达法 稍稍改变一下"我爱你"这一表达法，说句"我对你的爱与日俱增"能让你们彼此的感情有很大变化。如果你一遍又一遍地重复着"我爱你"，你的配偶可能会开始对之不以为然，而一种新的表达能让你们的关系有一种新鲜感。例如你可以对他这样表达你的爱："我真高兴我的生命里有你。"相信这句话能让他更感动，让你们感到更亲近。

❼ cue
/kjuː/
暗示,提示
❽ varation
/ˌveərɪˈeɪʃn/
n.变化，变动
❾ discount
/dɪsˈkaʊnt/
v.不重视，不理会

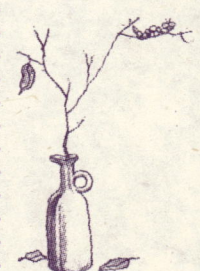

Love is not merchandise
爱情不是商品

Love is not a commodity; the real thing cannot be bought, sold, traded or stolen.

爱情并不是商品；真情实意不可能买到、卖掉、交换、或者偷走。

A reader apparently bruised[1] by some personal experience, writes in to complain, "If I steal a nickel's worth of merchandise, I am a thief and punished; but if I steal the love of another's wife, I am free."

This is a prevalent misconception in many people's minds—that love, like merchandise, can be "stolen." But love is not a commodity; the real thing cannot be bought, sold, traded or stolen. It is an act of the will, a turning of the emotions, a change in the climate of the personality.

When a husband or wife is "stolen" by another person, that husband or wife was already ripe for the stealing, was already predisposed[2] toward a new partner. The "love bandit" was only taking what was waiting to be taken, what wanted to be taken.

We tend to treat persons like goods. We even speak of children "belonging" to their parents. But nobody "belongs" to anyone else. Each person belongs to himself. Children are entrusted to their parents, and if their parents do not treat them properly, the state has a right to remove them from their parents' trusteeship[3].

Most of us, when young, had the experience of a sweet-heart being taken from us by somebody more attractive and more appealing. At the time, we may have resented this intruder —but as we grew older, we recognized that the sweet-heart had never been ours to begin with. It was not the intruder that "caused" the

一位读者显然是在个人经历上受过创伤，他写信抱怨道："如果我偷走了5分钱的商品，我就是个贼，要受到惩罚，但是如果我偷走了他人妻子的爱情，我没事儿。"

这是许多人心目中普遍存在的一种误解——爱情，像商品一样，可以偷走。但是爱情并不是商品；真情实意不可能买到、卖掉、交换、或者偷走。爱情是一种意志上的行为，是感情的转向，是个性上的变化。

当丈夫或妻子被另一个人"偷走"时，那个丈夫或妻子就已经具备了被偷走的条件，事先已经准备接受新的伴侣了。这位"爱情强盗"不过是取走等人取走、盼人取走的东西。

我们往往待人如物品。我们甚至说孩子"属于"父母；但是谁也不"属于"谁。每个人都属于自己。孩子是托付给父母的，如果父母不善待他们，政府有权取消父母对他们的托管身份。

我们多数人年轻时都有过恋人被某个更有魅力、更迷人的人抢走的经历。在当时，我们兴许怨恨这位不速之客——但是后来长大了，也就认识到了心上人本来就不属于我们。并不是不速之客"导致了"决裂，而是缺乏真正的感情。

❶ **bruise**
/bruːz/
vt. 打伤，损伤
❷ **predispose**
/ˌpriːdɪˈspəʊz/
vt. 使预先有倾向；使易接受
❸ **trusteeship**
/trʌsˈtiːʃɪp/
n. 托管人的身份

break, but the lack of a real relationship.

On the surface, many marriages seem to break up because of a "third party." This is, however, a psychological illusion. The other woman or the other man merely serve as a pretext[4] for dissolving a marriage that had already lost its essential integrity.

Nothing is more futile and more self-defeating than the bitterness of spurned[5] love, the vengeful feeling that someone else has "come between" oneself and a beloved. This is always a distortion of reality, for people are not the captives or victims of others— they are free agents, working out their own destinies for good or for ill.

But the rejected lover or mate can't afford to believe that his beloved has freely turned away from him— and so he ascribes[6] sinister[7] or magical properties to the interloper[8]. He calls him a hypnotist[9] or a thief or a home-breaker. In the vast majority of cases, however, when a home is broken, the breaking has begun long before any "third party" has appeared on the scene.

从表面上看，许多婚姻似乎是因为有了"第三者"才破裂的。然而这是一种心理上的错觉；另外那个女人，或者另外那个男人，无非是作为借口，用来解除早就不是完好无损的婚姻罢了。

因失恋而痛苦、因别人"插足"于自己与心上人之间而图报复是最徒劳、最自我折磨的。这种事总是歪曲了事实真相，因为谁都不是别人的俘虏或牺牲品——人都是自由行事的，不论命运是好是坏，都由自己来做主。

但是，遭离弃的情人或配偶无法相信他的心上人是主动地背离他的——因而他归咎于插足者心术不正或迷人有招。他把他叫做催眠师、窃贼或者破坏家庭的人。然而，从大多数事例看，一个家的破裂是早在什么"第三者"出现之前就开始了的。

❹ **pretext**
/ˈpriːtekst/
n. 借口

❺ **spurn**
/spɜːn/
vt. (formal)摒弃

❻ **ascribe...to**
(formal)归因于

❼ **sinister**
/ˈsɪnɪstə/
adj. 阴险的，邪恶的

❽ **interloper**
/ˈɪntələupə/
n. 闯入者

❾ **hypnotist**
/ˈhɪpnətɪst/
n. 催眠师

We are raising children, not flowers!
我们是在抚养孩子，不是在养花！

Our children's spirits are more important than any material things.

孩子的心灵比世上任何物质的东西都要重要。

David, my next-door neighbor, has two young kids aged five and seven. One day he was teaching his seven-year-old son Kelly how to push the lawn mower[1] around the yard. As he was teaching him how to turn the mower around at the end of the lawn, his wife, Jan, called to him to ask a question. As David turned to answer the question, Kelly pushed the lawn mower right through the flower bed at the edge of the lawn — leaving a two-foot wide path leveled to the ground!

When David turned back around and saw what had happened, he began to lose control. David had put a lot of time and effort into making those flower beds the envy[2] of the neighborhood. As he began to raise big voice to his son, Jan walked quickly over to him, put her hand on his shoulder and said, "David, please remember ... we're raising children, not flowers!"

Jan reminded me how important it is as a parent to remember our priorities[3]. Kids and their self-esteem[4] are more important than any physical object they might break or destroy. The window pane shattered[5] by a baseball, a lamp knocked over by a careless child, or a plate dropped in the kitchen are already broken. The flowers are already dead. We must remember not to add to the destruction by breaking a child's spirit and deadening his sense of liveliness.

Let's remember that our children's spirits are more important than any material things. When we do, self-esteem and love blossom[6] will grow more beautifully than any bed of flowers ever could.

我们是在抚养孩子，不是在养花！

我的邻居大卫有两个小孩，一个5岁，另一个7岁。一天，大卫正在教他7岁的儿子凯利如何使用割草机割草。当教到怎样在草坪尽头将割草机掉头时，他的妻子詹叫他问一些事情。当大卫转过身回答詹的问题时，凯利却把割草机推到了草坪边的花圃上——结果割草机所过之处，花尸遍地，原本美丽的花圃留下了一条两尺宽的小径。

大卫转过身，面对眼前的情景，怒不可遏。要知道，这个花圃花费了大卫多少时间和精力才侍弄成今天这个令邻居们无比羡慕的样子呀！他提高嗓门准备训斥凯利，这时詹快步走到他身边，用手轻轻地拍了拍他的肩膀，说："大卫，别忘了——我们是在养孩子，而不是在养花！"

詹的一番话提醒了我：作为父母我们应该清楚孩子和花究竟孰重孰轻。孩子以及他们的自尊要比被打破或损坏的任何东西都要重要得多啊！那些曾经被孩子们的棒球砸坏的窗户、不小心碰倒的台灯以及在厨房里掉在地上摔碎的碟子都是已经毁坏了的东西。正如花圃里被割掉的花再也不复存在了，我们就不要再去打破一个小孩子稚嫩纯净的心灵，使他们原本充满活力的感觉变得迟钝，乃至麻木。

孩子的心灵比世上任何物质的东西都要重要。只要我们牢记这一点，那么自尊心和爱的花朵就会比花圃中的任何花儿都开得灿烂、美丽。

---

❶ **lawn mower**
割草机
❷ **envy**
/ˈenvɪ/
n. 忌妒；羡慕
❸ **priority**
/praɪˈɒrətɪ/
n. 优先的事物
❹ **self-esteem**
/ˌself ɪˈstiːm/
n. 自尊
❺ **shatter**
/ˈʃætə/
v. 粉碎
❻ **blossom**
/ˈblɒsəm/
n. 花

Establish a sound relationship with your body
珍爱你的身体

Love all the parts of yourself, and if you can't love them, change them. If you can't change them, then accept them as they are.

珍爱你身体的每一部分吧！如果你无法珍爱它们，就改变它们；如果你无法改变它们，就接爱它们，面对现实。

"I find that when we really love and accept and approve of ourselves exactly as we are, then everything in life works."

——Louise Hay

The moment you arrived here on this Earth, you were given a body. The body you are given will be yours for the duration of your time here. Love it or hate it, accept it or reject it, it is the only one you will receive in this lifetime. It will be with you from the moment you draw your first breath to the last beat of your heart. Since there is a no-refund, no-exchange policy on this body, it is essential that you establish a sound relationship with it. So, the challenge here is to make peace with your body, and share its valuable lessons of acceptance and self-esteem[1]. If you are open to all these lessons, it can impart[2] to you valuable bits of wisdom that will guide you along your path of life.

Acceptance Acceptance is the act of embracing what life presents to you with a good attitude. Unfortunately, for many people, their body is the target for their harshest judgments and the barometer by which they measure their self-worth. They hold themselves up to an unattainable standard and berate[3] themselves for failure of perfection. Imposing harsh judgments on your body limits the range of experiences you allow yourself to enjoy. How many times has a potentially wonderful day at the beach been spoiled by your judgments about how you look in a bathing suit? Imagine how liberating it would be to happily walk across the warm sand without feeling self-conscious.

"我发现当我们真正喜爱、接受、欣赏原原本本的自我时,生活就会事事顺心、万事如意。"

——路易斯·黑

从你来到世上的那一刻起,你就拥有了一个身体。在你的有生之年,这个身体就是属于你的。爱也好,恨也罢,不管你接受与否,它是你一生拥有的惟一。从你的第一次呼吸到最后一次心跳,这个身体都与你同在。既然这个身体无法退换,那么至关重要的就是要珍爱它。因此,这里的挑战就是认同你的身体,并接受其宝贵的课程:自我认可和自尊自重。如果你乐于学习所有这些课程,你将会从中得到宝贵的智慧启迪,引导你在人生旅途上一路走好。

自我认可 所谓自我认可是指欣然接受生活所赋予你的一切。然而不幸的是,许多人都对自己的身体十分苛求,百般挑剔,以它作为衡量自身价值的标志。他们往往给自己设立一个不可企及的标准,而后又因达不到完美而深感自责。其实,对身体的过于苛求挑剔限制了你享受生活的范围。想想有多少次你本可以在海滩上尽情享受,却因为你担心自己穿着泳衣的样子而顾虑重重,浪费了大好时光?试想一下那种自由自在的感觉

❶ **self-esteem**
/ˌself ɪˈstiːm/
n. 自尊,自重

❷ **impart**
/ɪmˈpɑːt/
vt. (formal) 给予,赋予

❸ **berate**
/bɪˈreɪt/
vt. 严厉指责

I have a friend who dreams of learning to scuba dive[4], but refuses to even try, because she worries about how she would look swaddled[5] in a tight rubber wet suit. What a pity! Though a good sense of self-acceptance would allow her, and you, to fully participate in all aspects of life, without reservation, immediately. You know you are moving in the right direction when you can accept your body exactly as it is in its present form. True acceptance comes when you can appreciate your body as it is, and no longer feel that you need to alter it to be worthy of someone's love—most especially your own. Of course, it doesn't mean that you should never endeavor to[6] improve your body, or that you have to be resigned to [7]what you have been given. What this does mean, however, is that you need to stop criticizing, finding fault with your body. The drive for self-improvement is completely healthy as long as it comes from a place of self-love rather than a feeling of self-contempt[8]. Love all the parts of yourself, and if you can't love them, change them. If you can't change them, then accept them as they are.

Don't you know The Special Olympics are filled with people who have accepted their bodies despite obvious handicaps? As to your body, you can either continue to complain bitterly and immerse yourself in self-deprecation[9], or you can make the mental shift into acceptance. Either way, the reality remains the same. Acceptance or rejection of your body only carries weight in your mind; it has no bearings on how you actually look, so why not choose the ease of acceptance rather than the pain of rejection? The choice is yours.

吧！漫步在暖暖的沙滩上，轻松快乐，不为自己的样子而忸怩不安。

我有一位朋友，她非常想学斯库巴潜水却执意不肯尝试，因为她担心自己穿着湿漉漉的紧身橡胶衣的样子会很难看。这真遗憾，其实，只要有良好的自我认可意识，她，还有你，就能全身心地直接参与生活的各个方面。如果你能现实地接受你所拥有的身体，那就对了。当你不再感到需要改变你的身体以取悦某人（尤其是你自己），而是懂得去欣赏它时，你就学会了真正的自我认可。当然，这并不是说你应该听天由命，放弃改善自身条件的努力。但是，需要强调的一点是，你不应该对你的身体吹毛求疵，百般挑剔。自我改善的需求是完全健康有益的，只要它是出于自尊自爱的动机，而不是自轻自贱的念头。珍爱你身体的每一部分吧！如果你无法珍爱它们，就改变它们；如果你无法改变它们，就接受它们，面对现实。

知道残奥会吗？那里的人们有着各种明显的身体残疾，但是他们都能够接受认可自己的身体。对于你的身体，你可以无休止地抱怨，终日自惭形秽；也可以从心理上来个转变，去接受它。无论你做何选择，你的身体现状都不会有任何改变。接受或拒绝你的

❹ scuba dive
斯库巴潜水
❺ swaddle
/ˈswɒdl/
vt. 包住，缠住
❻ endeavor to
努力
❼ be resigned to
听从，顺从
❽ self-contempt
/self kənˈtempt/
n. 自轻自贱
❾ self-depreciation
/self dɪˌpriːʃɪˈeɪʃn/
n. 自贬，自惭形秽

Self-Esteem Self-esteem is feeling worthy and able to meet life's challenges. It is as essential as the air we breathe, and just as intangible[10]. It comes from the depths of our core[11], yet it is reflected in every single outward action we take, grand or small. It is the essence from which we measure our worth and the most important building block in the foundation of our intangible. If self-esteem is a lesson that you need to learn, you will be tested over and over until you feel confident about who you are and believe in your intrinsic value. Mind you, do not measure your worth by external appearance. Looks will change and fade—ultimately[12] being an unreliable source of self-esteem, while your true inner self will always be with you—actually being the underlying[13] source of self-esteem.

身体现状，只会影响你的心情，而和你的实际形象毫无关系。既然如此，何不卸下无视现实的痛苦而轻轻松松地接受它呢？这全由你来决定。

自尊自重 所谓自尊自重是指相信自身的价值以及接受人生挑战的能力。自尊自重就如同我们所呼吸的空气一样，不可或缺，却又是无形的。它来源于心灵深处，却体现在我们外在的一言一行，一举一动之间。它是衡量自身价值的实质所在，也是心灵成长最重要的奠基石。自尊自重是你必修的一门课程。在人生的道路上，你将一再受到测试、考验，直到你能够接受现实的自我，并相信自身的内在价值。切记：不要以外在的身体面貌来衡量自身的价值。人的外表是会改变的，日渐衰老憔悴，所以根本不能成为自尊自重的可靠源泉，而你真正的内在自我将永远与你同在，它才真正是你自尊自重的根本。

⑩ **intangible**
/ɪn'tændʒəbl/
adj.不可触摸的；无形的

⑪ **core**
/kɔː/
n.核心部份

⑫ **ultimately**
/'ʌltɪmətlɪ/
adv.最后

⑬ **underlying**
/ˌʌndə'laɪɪŋ/
adj.深层的，根本的

Please dress me in red
请给我穿上红色的衣服

She comforted him by telling Tyler that she was dying too, and that she would be with him soon in heaven.

她安慰泰勒说,她也将要离开人世,不久会和他在天堂见面。

In my dual¹ profession as an educator and health care provider, I have worked with numerous children infected with the virus that causes AIDS. The relationships that I have had with these special kids have been gifts in my life. They have taught me so many things, but I have especially learned that great courage can be found in the smallest of packages. Let me tell you about Tyler.

Tyler was born infected with HIV; his mother was also infected. From the very beginning of his life, he was dependent on medications to enable him to survive. When he was five, he had a tube surgically inserted in a vein in his chest. This tube was connected to a pump, which he carried in a small backpack on his back. Medications were hooked up² to this pump and were continuously supplied through this tube to his blood stream. At times, he also needed supplemented oxygen to support his breathing.

Tyler wasn't willing to give up one single moment of his childhood to this deadly disease. It was not unusual to find him playing and racing around his backyard, wearing his medicine-laden backpack and dragging his tank of oxygen behind him in his little wagon. All of us who knew Tyler marveled at his pure joy in being alive and the energy it gave him. Tyler's mom often teased him by telling him that he moved so fast she needed to dress him in red. That way, when she peered through the window to check on him playing in the yard, she could quickly spot him.

This dreaded disease eventually wore down³ even the likes of

作为一名教育和健康护理工作者，我曾经和数不清的感染上艾滋病病毒的孩子打过交道。我和这些特殊的孩子之间的关系是生活赋予我的恩赐。他们教会我许多东西，我尤其懂得了即使在最弱小的人物身上也能发现其所蕴涵的巨大勇气。让我告诉你泰勒的故事吧。

泰勒出生时就从母体感染上了艾滋病病毒。自他来到人间就一直靠药物维持生命。他5岁时做手术，胸部插了一根管子，管子连着他背的背包里的泵。泵不断地把药通过管子输入他的血液。有时他还需要补充氧气帮助呼吸。

泰勒不愿因这种致命的疾病而放弃童年的一分一秒。经常能发现他背着装药的背包、拖着载有氧气罐的小车在他家后院玩耍奔跑。我们所有认识泰勒的人都惊叹于生命带给他的那种淳朴的欢乐和赋予他的活力。泰勒的妈妈经常逗他说，他跑得太快了，得给他穿件红衣服。这样，当她透过窗户看他在院子里玩得怎样时，就能很快找到他了。

可怕的疾病最终拖垮了精力充沛得像小电动机似的泰勒。他的病情越来越严重，不幸的是，身染艾滋病病毒的妈妈也病入膏肓。

❶ dual
/ˈdjuːəl/
adj. 双重的
❷ hook up
把(部件)装接起来
❸ wear down
使筋疲力尽,使消瘦

a little dynamo[4] like Tyler. He grew quite ill and, unfortunately, so did his HIV-infected mother. When it became apparent that he wasn't going to survive, Tyler's mom talked to him about death. She comforted him by telling Tyler that she was dying too, and that she would be with him soon in heaven.

A few days before his death, Tyler beckoned[5] me over to his hospital bed and whispered, "I might die soon. I'm not scared. When I die, please dress me in red, Mom promised she's coming to heaven, too. I'll be playing when she gets there, and I want to make sure she can find me."

泰勒即将离开人世时,妈妈和他谈起死亡。她安慰他说,她也将要离开人世,不久会和他在天堂见面。

　　泰勒病逝前几天,招呼我到他病床前,低声对我说,"我可能就要死了,我不害怕。我死时,请给我穿上红色的衣服。妈妈答应我她也会来天堂,她来的时候我会在玩,我得保证她能找到我。"

❹ **dynamo**
/ˈdaɪnəməʊ/
n. 发电机,发动机

❺ **beckon**
/ˈbekən/
vt. 示意,召唤

Sand and stone
伤害只写在沙地上

When someone hurts us we should write it down in sand where winds of forgiveness can erase it away.

受到伤害时，我们应该把它记在沙地上，宽恕之风将其抹平。

The story goes that two friends were walking through the desert. During some point of the journey they had an argument, and one friend slapped[1] the other one in the face.

The one who got slapped was hurt, but without saying anything, wrote in the sand: "Today my best friend slapped me in the face."

They kept on walking until they found an oasis[2], where they decided to take a bath. The one who had been slapped got stuck in the mire[3] and started drowning[4], but the friend saved him.

After he recovered from the near drowning, he wrote on a stone: "Today my best friend saved my life."

The friend who had slapped and saved his best friend asked him, "After I hurt you, you wrote in the sand and now you write on a stone. Why?"

The other friend replied: "When someone hurts us we should write it down in sand where winds of forgiveness[5] can erase[6] it away. But when someone does something good for us, we must engraves[7] it in stone where no wind ever erases it."

LEARN TO WRITE YOUR HURTS IN THE SAND AND TO CARVE YOUR BENEFITS IN STONE.

两个朋友在荒漠里穿行，途中他们发生了争执；其中一个人扇了另一位一个耳光。

被打的人非常伤心，但他什么也没说，只是在沙地上写道："今天，我最好的朋友打了我一个耳光。"

他们继续往前走，发现了一片绿洲，他们决定在那里洗个澡。结果，被打的那位陷进了泥潭，眼看就要被淹死，但他的朋友救了他。

恢复过来后，他在石头上写道："今天，我最好的朋友救了我的命。"

那位打他并救了他的朋友问，"为什么我伤害你时，你把字写在沙地上，而现在却把字刻在石头上呢？"

被救的那位答道："受到伤害时，我们应该把它记在沙地上，宽恕之风会将其抹平。可受人恩惠时，我们应该把它刻在石头上，任何风雨也不会把它擦掉。"

学会将所受的伤害写在沙子上，把所得的恩泽刻在石头上。

有人这样说，找到一个特别的人只需要用一分钟，欣赏他需要用一小时，喜欢他需要用一天，但忘掉他却需要用一生的时间。

把这句话送给那些你永远无法忘记的人

❶ **slap**
/slæp/
vt. 用巴掌打

❷ **oasis**
/əʊˈeɪsɪs/
n. 绿洲

❸ **mire**
/ˈmaɪə/
n. 泥潭

❹ **drown**
/draʊn/
v. 淹死

❺ **forgiveness**
/fəˈɡɪvnɪs/
n. 宽恕

❻ **erase**
/ɪˈreɪz/
v. 擦掉；抹去

❼ **engrave**
/ɪnˈɡreɪv/
v. 雕刻

They say it takes a minute to find a special person, an hour to appreciate[8] them, a day to love them, but an entire[9] life to forget them.

Send this phrase to the people you'll never forget. It's a short message to let them know that you'll never forget them.

Take the time to live.

吧。这段短短的话能让他们知道你永远不会忘记他们。

此生不忘。

❽ **appreciate**
/ə'priːʃɪeɪt/
v. 了解并欣赏

❾ **entire**
/ɪn'taɪə/
adj. 整个的；完整的

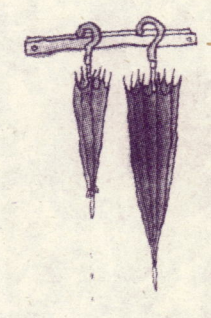

A full-time school called life
生活是一所全日制学校

Life is not, in fact, fair, and you may indeed have a more difficult life path than others around you, deserved or not.

生活其实并不公平,也许命运不该如此安排,但你的一生就是可能比你周围的人艰难、坎坷。

You are enrolled in a full-time school called "life." Each day in this school you will have the opportunity to learn lessons. You may like the lessons or hate them, but you have designed them as part of your curriculum[1].

Why are you here? What is your purpose? Humans have sought to discover the meaning of life for a very long time. What we and our ancestors have overlooked, however, is that there is no one answer. The meaning of life is different for every individual.

Each person has his or her own purpose and distinct path, unique and separate from anyone else's. As you travel your life path, you will be presented with numerous lessons that you will need to learn in order to fulfill that purpose. The lessons you are presented with are specific to you; learning these lessons is the key to discovering and fulfilling the meaning and relevance[2] of your own life.

As you travel through your lifetime, you may encounter challenging lessons that others don't have to face, while others spend years struggling with challenges that you don't need to deal with. You may never know why you are blessed with a wonderful marriage, while your friends suffer through bitter arguments and painful divorces, just as you cannot be sure why you struggle financially while your peers enjoy abundance[3]. The only thing you can count on for certain is that you will be presented with all the lessons that you specifically need to learn; whether you choose to learn them or not is entirely up to[4] you.

生活是一所全日制学校，而你则是这里的学生。在这所学校里，每天你都有机会学习到各种课程；不管你是否喜欢，这些课程都将是你必修的内容。

你为什么会在这个世上？你的生活目的是什么？很长时期以来，人们从未停止过对人生意义的探索。但是，我们和我们的祖先都忽视了这样一个事实，即人生的意义因人而异，根本没一个确定的答案。

人各有志，各人的人生目的和道路都独一无二，各不相同。在人生旅途上，你需要不断地学习知识、接受教训，以期有朝一日实现你的人生目的。你所要学习的内容是专门为你量身定制的；而认真学习这些经验、教训则是探索人生意义、实现人生目的的关键。

在你的人生旅途中，你也许会面临别人无需面对的挑战和教训；当然，你也无需应付别人为之奋战多年的各种挑战。你也许永远弄不懂为什么你能幸运地拥有美好婚姻，而你的朋友却饱受婚姻不和之苦，离婚之痛；同样，你也无法明白为什么你生活拮据、疲于谋生，而你的朋友却生活优裕。但是有一点你可以确信无疑，即你将有缘见识你所注定要学的知识和经验；至于你是否乐意学习，

❶ curriculum
/kəˈrɪkjʊləm/
n. (学校的) 全部课程,必修课程
❷ relevance
/ˈreləvəns/
n. 意义
❸ abundance
/əˈbʌndəns/
n. 富足,充裕
❹ up to sb.
取决于某人

The challenge here, therefore, is to align yourself with[5] your own unique path by learning individual lessons. This is one of the most difficult challenges you will be faced with in your lifetime, as sometimes your path will be radically[6] different from others. But, remember, don't compare your path to the people around you and focus on the disparity[7] between their lessons and yours. You need to remember that you will only be faced with lessons that you are capable of learning and are specific to your own growth.

Our sense of fairness is the expectation of equity[8]—the assumption that all things are equal and that justice will always prevail. Life is not, in fact, fair, and you may indeed have a more difficult life path than others around you, deserved or not. Everyone's circumstances are unique, and everyone needs to handle his or her own circumstances differently. If you want to move toward serenity[9], yon will be required to move out of the complaining phase of "it's not fair". Focusing on the unfairness of circumstances keeps you comparing yourself with others rather than appreciating your own special uniqueness. You miss out on learning your individual lessons by distracting yourself with feelings of bitterness and resentment.

则完全是你自己的选择。

由此可见，这里的挑战在于你要汲取各种不同的经验和教训以使自己的生活符合自己独特的人生道路。这是你终生需要面对的最严峻的挑战，因为有时你的人生道路会与别人的截然不同。但是，切记不要拿你的人生道路和你周围的人的相比，计较不同的经验和教训；切记你所要学习的是你力所能及的，并且是为你的成长所特设的。

我们总是期望事事公正、人人平等，这就是所谓的公平感。但是，生活其实并不公平，也许命运不该如此安排，但你的一生就是可能比你周围的人艰难、坎坷。每个人的境况各不相同，因此对待自己的境遇也需要有不同的方法。要想寻求心灵的平静，你必须摆脱抱怨世道不公的心态。过分计较世事不公会使你自轻自贱，看不到自己的独特之处。由于愤世懊恼情绪的干扰，你可能错过学习自己该学的课程。

❺ **align...with**
使⋯⋯一致
❻ **radically**
/ˈrædɪklɪ/
adv. 完全地，彻底地
❼ **disparity**
/dɪˈspærɪtɪ/
n. 差异，悬殊
❽ **equity**
/ˈekwətɪ/
n. 公平，公正
❾ **serenity**
/səˈrenɪtɪ/
n. 宁静，无忧无虑

There are no mistakes, only lessons
没有错误,只有教训

You should force yourself to see the bigger picture, by so doing, you will be able to shift the focus away from the anger and resentment.

你必须强迫自己看得更广阔些,只有这样你才能转移你的注意力,不至于沉溺于怒火和仇恨之中。

Human growth is a process of experimentation, trial, and error, ultimately leading to wisdom. Each time you choose to trust yourself and take action, you can never quite be certain how the situation will turn out. Sometimes you are victorious, and sometimes you become disillusioned[1]. The failed experiments, however, are no less valuable than the experiments that ultimately prove successful; in fact, you usually learn more from your perceived "failures" than you do from your perceived "successes".

If you have made what you perceive to be a mistake, or failed to live up to your own expectations, you will most likely put up a barrier between your essence and the part of you that is the alleged wrong-doer. However, perceiving past actions as mistakes implies guilt and blame, and it is not possible to learn anything meaningful while you are engaged in blaming. Therefore, forgiveness is required when you are harshly judging yourself.

Forgiveness is the act of erasing an emotional debt. There are four kinds of forgiveness.

The first is beginner forgiveness for yourself.

The second kind of forgiveness is beginner forgiveness for another.

The third kind of forgiveness is advanced forgiveness of yourself. This is for serious transgressions[2], the ones you carry with deep shame. When you do something that violates[3] your own

人的成长是一个不断尝试，不断经历失误，最终获得智慧的过程。每当你充满信心采取行动时，你永远无法预见会有什么样的结果，或成功，或失望。不论最终成功与否，这些尝试都是可贵的；事实上，你往往可以从失败的经历中学到更多的东西。

当你自责犯了某个错误，或辜负了自己的期望时，你往往会在你的真正自我和所谓的"犯错嫌疑人"之间竖起一道障碍。然而，如果你认为过去的行为是错误，这势必会让你内疚、自责；而当你忙着自责时，你根本无暇顾及从中汲取任何有益的东西。因此，你对自己过分苛求之时也正是你需要宽恕自己的时候。

宽恕是指宽大为怀，尽释前嫌。有四种类型的宽恕。

第一种是对自己的初级宽恕。

第二种是对他人的初级宽恕，即你需要宽恕他人的过失。

第三种是对自己更深层次的宽恕，所涉及的是那些你深感耻辱的严重过失。当你做了某件违背自己的价值观和道德观的事情，你的实际行为和你的为人准则之间就出现了一道裂缝。这时，你需要努力去原谅自己的过失，以便修复这道裂缝，重新找回真正的

---

❶ **disillusion**
/ˌdɪsɪˈluːʒn/
vt. 使幻想破灭

❷ **transgression**
/trænzˈɡreʃn/
n. 坏事，违反道德的事

❸ **violate**
/ˈvaɪəleɪt/
v. 违反，违背

values and ethics, you create a chasm[4] between your standards and your actual behavior. In such a case, you need to work very hard at forgiving yourself for these deeds so that you call close this chasm and realign with the best part of yourself. This does not mean that you should rush to forgive yourself or not feel regret or remorse; but wallowing in these feelings for a protracted[5] period of time is not healthy, and punishing yourself excessively will only creates a bigger gap between you and your ethics.

The last and perhaps most difficult one is the advanced forgiveness of another. At some time of our life, you may have been severely wronged or hurt by another person to such a degree that forgiveness seems impossible. However, harboring[6] resentment and revenge fantasies only keeps you trapped[7] in victimhood. Under such a circumstance, you should force yourself to see the bigger picture, by so doing, you will be able to shift the focus away from the anger and resentment. It is only through forgiveness that you can erase wrongdoing and clean the memory. When you can finally release the situation, you may come to see it as a necessary part of your growth.

自我。这并不意味着你可以很随意地原谅自己或不知悔恨、一错再错；但是，一味地深陷于自责、悔恨是不健康的，而且过分的自我惩罚只会使你越发远离你的道德标准。

  第四种也是最难的一种宽恕，则是对他人的更深层次的宽恕。生活中，有时你可能受到了极大的委屈、极深的伤害，而且这一切似乎是不可原谅的。但是，如果你的心中充满仇恨以及复仇的幻想，那你只会深陷于受伤害的情绪之中，不可自拔。此时，你必须强迫自己看得更广阔些，只有这样你才能转移你的注意力，不至于沉溺于怒火和仇恨之中。只有通过宽恕，你才能忘却过错，重新获得心灵的平静。当你最终能够从中解脱，你也许会意识到这是你成长过程中必修的一课。

❹ **chasm**
/ˈkæzəm/
n. 裂缝

❺ **protracted**
/prəˈtræktɪd/
adj. 拖延的, 延续的

❻ **harbor**
/ˈhɑːbə/
v. 心怀

❼ **trap**
/træp/
v. 使落入圈套

Win-win contract
双赢的协定

No one likes being bossed or dictated to, let alone defeated.

没有人愿意被管束或被命令,更不用说被击败了。

I am often reminded that the path to progress is not victory but compromise. For all to benefit, all must give. Compromise, however, sounds wrong—weak and indecent. Strong men, and strong women, stand firm; they brook[1] no middle way for that is to admit defeat. That was the way that I, too, used to think. Convert them to my view, impose my will, dictate my terms; that way they would know who was boss. The trouble is that no one likes being bossed or dictated to, let alone defeated, so any deal I arranged could never be relied on; when the cat was away, the mice would undoubtedly play. The deals that work, I came to learn, are the deals where each party thinks that they won—"win-win contract" they are sometimes called.

Obviously, perhaps, but the idea was a hard one for me to grasp. I had been brought up to fight my corner to the bitter end; success meant beating the opposition, which included even my own colleagues half of the time. It made for a world of envy, in-fighting[2], and suspicion. I lived life on a seesaw[3]— jousting[4] against my opposites, sometimes up and sometimes down; very energetic, but ultimately going nowhere, when it ought to have been at least a carriage going somewhere.

You live and you learn. That turns out to be the key: we have to turn our competitors into partners if we want the deals to stick and the world to move, and you have to find a shared ambition for all those partners to justify their compromises. "Peace and Prosperity for All" will do very nicely at this time of year.

我常常留意到，要想事情有所进展，我们不能处处求胜而要学会妥协。为了共赢，大家都必须有所放弃。然而，妥协听起来总不大对劲——它代表懦弱和鄙俗。坚定的人们总是坚守自己的立场，他们从来不能忍受折中的办法，因为那意味着承认失败。我过去也是如此认为的。所以我总是要别人接纳我的观点，把自己的意愿强加给他们，或是态度强硬地提出我的条件。我以为只有这样，他们才会知道谁是头儿。问题在于，没有人愿意被管束或被命令，更不用说被击败了。所以，以上我采取的任何一种方式绝不可靠。毫无疑问，山中无老虎，猴子称大王。我开始懂得，真正切实可行的处理方式是让所有相关的人都认为他们是赢家——人们有时称之为"双赢的协定"。

道理可能显而易见，但对我而言，真正懂得它却不是轻而易举的。我从小就被教导要为保障自己的利益和地位奋战到底；成功意味着击败对手，其中甚至常常包括我自己的同事。这种对立的态度导致了没完没了的妒忌、暗斗和猜疑。我仿佛生活在跷跷板的一端，挥舞着长矛与另一端的对手进行格斗。时而上扬，时而下挫；充满着活力与变化，但最终却没有了目的和方向。然而，生活最

❶ **brook**
/brʊk/
vt. 容忍，忍受
❷ **infighting**
/ˈɪnfaɪtɪŋ/
n. 激烈竞争
❸ **seesaw**
/ˈsiːsɔː/
n. 跷跷板
❹ **joust**
/dʒaʊst/
v. 骑马用长矛比武(打斗)

And, of course we were told to love our enemies. I used to think that both silly and impossible. Now I see that if we want to forge[5] a lasting win-win contract, or to change a seesaw for a carriage going somewhere, then we have to learn to make our adversaries[6] our allies[7].

起码该像一辆马车,有终点和目标。

我们在生活中学会生活。事实证明问题的答案或关键在于:如果我们想要持久有效地处理问题,让事情得以顺利进行,那我们就必须化干戈为玉帛,为所有伙伴寻求共同的目标,让他们有充分的达成妥协和解的理由。"为所有人谋求和平与富足"的原则在我们这个时代必定会大行其道。

当然,我们早就被告知要爱我们的敌人。我过去认为这不仅愚蠢而且不切实际。今天我才明白,我们若要订立一个持久的双赢协定,或要将"跷跷板"改造成为有着一定目标和方向的马车,就必须学会将敌手变为盟友。

❺ **forge**
/fɔːdʒ/
vt. 建立

❻ **adversary**
/ˈædvəsəri/
n. 敌手;对手

❼ **ally**
/ˈælaɪ/
n. 联盟者;盟友

Mule in the well
井 底 之 骡

The adversities that come along to bury us usually have within them the very real potential to benefit us!

通常，在那些发生在我们身上且要葬送我们的逆境中，都确实同时潜藏着对我们有利的因素。

This parable is told of a farmer who owned an old mule. The mule fell into the farmer's well. The farmer heard the mule praying or whatever mules do when they fall into wells. After carefully assessing the situation, the farmer sympathized with the mule, but decided that neither the mule nor the well was worth the trouble of saving. Instead, he called his neighbors together, told them what had happened, and enlisted[1] them to help haul dirt to bury the old mule in the well and put him out of his misery.

Initially the old mule was hysterical! But as the farmer and his neighbors continued shoveling[2] and the dirt hit his back, a thought struck him. It suddenly <u>dawned on</u>[3] him that every time a shovel load of dirt landed on his back, he would shake it off and step up!

This he did, blow after blow. "Shake it off and step up shake it off and step up...shake it off and step up! " He repeated to encourage himself. No matter how painful the blows, or how distressing[4] the situation seemed, the old mule fought panic[5] and just kept right on shaking it off and stepping up!

It wasn't long before the old mule, battered and exhausted, stepped triumphantly[6] over the wall of that well! What seemed like it would bury him actually helped him all because of the manner in which he handled his adversity[7].

THAT'S LIFE! If we face our problems and respond to them positively, and refuse to give in to panic, bitterness, or self-pity.

这个故事讲的是一个农夫，他有一头老骡子。有一天，老骡子掉进了农夫的井里。农夫听到了老骡子在祈祷，做着骡子掉进井后通常会做的事情。农夫仔细斟酌过情势之后，虽然同情这头老骡子，但还是认为不值得费力去解救这头老骡子，也不值得去保留这口井。于是，他把邻居们叫来，告诉他们所发生的事情，并让他们帮忙搬运泥土把这头老骡子埋在井里，以解除它的痛苦。

刚开始时，老骡子歇斯底里，激动异常。但当农夫和邻居们不停地把土铲落到它身上时，它的脑海中闪过一个念头。它突然意识到，每当一铲土打落在它背上时，它都可以把土抖掉，再踏上去。

就这样，它一次又一次地重复着，不停地给自己鼓气："把土抖掉，再踏上去……把土抖掉，再踏上去……把土抖掉，再踏上去！"不管泥土砸在身上有多痛，也不管情况看起来是何等地难熬，这头老骡子竭力排除心里的恐慌，只是一直坚持把土抖掉，再踏上去。

没多久，这头伤痕累累、疲惫不堪的老骡子就昂首挺胸地跨出了井沿！而事实上解救它的正是看起来要它命的困境——这都要归功于它处理逆境的方式。

❶ **enlist**
/ɪnˈlɪst/
vt. 获得(帮助，支持等)

❷ **shovel**
/ˈʃʌvəl/
vt. 铲，铲起

❸ **dawn on sb.**
明白，了解

❹ **distressing**
/dɪˈstresɪŋ/
adj. 使人痛苦的

❺ **panic**
/ˈpænɪk/
n. 惊慌

❻ **triumphantly**
/traɪˈʌmfntlɪ/
adv. 成功地；得意扬扬地

❼ **adversity**
/ədˈvɜːsətɪ/
n. 逆境；厄运

———— 人 生 篇

The adversities that come along to bury us usually have within them the very real potential to benefit us!

Never be afraid to try something new. Remember that amateurs[8] built the ark[9]. Professionals built the Titanic.

生活就是如此！只要我们能正视困难并能积极应对困难，不屈服于恐慌、痛苦或自怨自艾。

通常，在那些发生在我们身上且要葬送我们的逆境中，都确实同时潜藏着对我们有利的因素。

永远不要害怕新尝试。记住生手照样能做出一叶方舟，只不过行家建造的是泰坦尼克号罢了。

❽ amateur
/ˈæmətə/
n. 业余爱好者

❾ ark
/ɑːk/
n. 方舟

The richest woman in the world
世上最富有的女人

I came to realize more than ever before that the love of my true companion makes me rich beyond anything material a man could ever give to me.

我比以往更加清醒地意识到,我的爱侣给予了我一个男人所能给予的比任何物质更为宝贵的财富。

I just spent four days with a girlfriend who is married to a very wealthy man. He gave her a $35,000 ruby[1] ring as an engagement present. He gave her a $25,000 emerald[2] necklace for Mother's Day. He gave her $250,000 to redecorate their enormous home on five acres of land. Her bathroom cost $120,000 to build. Even her dog eats from a silver-plated dish engraved with his name.

Her husband has taken her all over the world — Tahiti for sun, Paris for clothes, London for the theater, Australia for adventure. There is nowhere she cannot go, nothing she cannot buy, nothing she cannot have— except for one thing: He does not love her the way she wants to be loved.

We sat in her study late last night, my friend and I, talking as only women who have known each other since they were just girls can talk. We talked about our bodies, changing with each passing year, hers now rounded with the new life she was carrying inside. And we talked about our men—her wealthy, successful financier, my hardworking, struggling artist.

"Are you happy?" I asked her. She sat quietly for a moment, toying with the three-carat diamond wedding ring on her finger. Then, slowly, almost in a whisper, she began to explain. She appreciated all of her wealth, but she would trade it in a minute for a certain quality of love she didn't feel with her husband. She loved him intellectually more than she felt her love for him. She did not respect many of his values in life, and this turned her off to him

世上最富有的女人

我刚和一位女友共度了4天。她嫁给一个有钱人。他送给她的订婚礼物是价值35,000美元的红宝石戒指。母亲节时,他送给她价值25,000美元的翡翠项链。他给她250,000美元来重新装修他们占地5英亩的豪宅。她的浴室就花费了120,000美元来修建。就连她的宠物狗都用刻有他名字的镀银餐盘进食。

她丈夫带她游遍了世界各地——到塔希提日光浴,到巴黎买时装,到伦敦看戏剧,到澳大利亚探险。没有她不能去的地方,没有她买不到的东西,她什么都有——除了一样东西:他没有如她所愿地爱她。

昨天深夜,我和女友坐在她的书房中说话,聊着只有从小就相识的女伴之间才会有的梯己话。我们谈论着随岁月变化着的身体,如今她因怀有了新生命而身体日渐滚圆。我们还谈起我们的丈夫——她那富有而成功的金融家和我那勤奋而艰难营生的艺术家。

"你幸福吗?"我问她。她静静地坐在那儿,摆弄着手指上三克拉的钻石婚戒。过了一会儿,她才慢慢地,几乎是用耳语低声向我道来。她对她所拥有的财富心存感激,但她却愿意立刻用这些财富来换取一份爱——她所渴望的那种爱,这种爱是她无法从丈夫那里得到的。她对他的爱更多的是理智上的,

❶ ruby
/ˈruːbɪ/
n. 红宝石

❷ emerald
/ˈemərəld/
n. 绿宝石,悲翠

sexually. Although he was fully committed to her, and took care of her, he did not give her the experience of being loved from moment to moment — the affection, the tenderness, the words lovers use, the listening, the sensitivity, the nurturing, the respect, the willingness to participate with her in creating the relationship each day.

As I listened to my friend, I came to realize more than ever before that the love of my true companion makes me rich beyond anything material a man could ever give to me. This was not the first time I have deeply felt this, but once again, it was a reminder of my great good fortune.

And I thought about the drawerful of cards and love notes written by him. I thought about him touching me, grasping my hand protectively as we cross the street, stroking[3] my hair as I lie in his lap, kissing me all over my face when I correctly guess his charades[4]. I thought about the adventures our minds go on together, exploring ideas and concepts, understanding our past, glimpsing our future. I thought about our trust and our respect, our hunger for life and learning.

And in this moment, I saw that my friend envied me and my relationship. She, who sat in her luxurious home, wrapped in jewels and splendor[5], envied our vitality, our playfulness[6], our passion, our commitment— yes, our commitment.

For in that moment, I saw that what we have that is greater

而不是内心的感受。她不欣赏他的许多价值观，这使她厌烦和他的性生活。尽管他对她绝对忠诚，悉心地照顾她，他仍无法给予她那种时时刻刻被爱的感觉——那种浓情蜜意、体贴温柔、情人间的贴心软语、用心聆听、敏感细腻、关怀备至、相互尊重以及每天和她经营这份感情的意愿。

听了她的诉说，我比以往更加清醒地意识到，我的爱侣给予了我一个男人所能给予的比任何物质更为宝贵的财富。我并非第一次有这种深刻的感觉，而此时我又想起了自己所拥有的巨大财富。

我想到满抽屉他写的卡片和情书。我想起了他的爱抚，想起了他牵着我的手，护着我过马路，想起了我躺在他的膝上时，他轻抚我的秀发，想起了当我猜出他的字谜时，他吻遍我的脸庞。我还想起了我们共同的思想历程，探讨各种想法和观念，理解我们的过去、展望我们的未来。我想到了我们之间的信任和尊重以及对生活和知识的渴望。

在这一刻，我看到我的朋友对我和我的婚姻羡慕万分。她虽然身居豪宅、穿金戴银，却羡慕我们的活力、我们的乐趣、我们的热情以及承诺——是的，我们的承诺。

因为在那一刻，我明白了我们之间所拥

❸ **stroke**
/strəʊk/
vt. 抚摸

❹ **charade**
/ʃəˈrɑːd/
n. 字谜

❺ **splendor**
/ˈsplendə/
n. 豪华，奢华

❻ **playfulness**
/ˈpleɪflnɪs/
n. 乐趣

than anything else between us is commitment: to loving one another fully, completely, as deeply as we know how for as long as we can. In that moment I learned the difference between having money and truly being wealthy. And I knew that I was already the richest woman in the world.

有的最珍贵的便是承诺:承诺尽我们所能,全身心地,竭尽全力地一直深爱对方。在那一刻,我懂得了拥有金钱和拥有真正的财富之间的差异。我知道我早已是世上最富有的女人了。

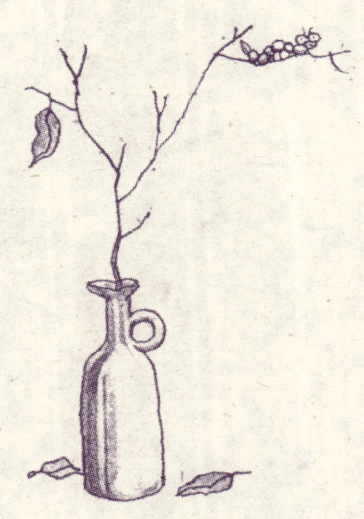

"There" is no better than "here"
彼岸无尽头,知足才常乐

Gratitude fills your heart with the joyful feeling and allows you to fully appreciate everything that arises on your path.

心存感恩,你的心灵就会充满愉悦,你就能真正领会人生路上的种种体验。

Many people believe that they will be happy once they arrive at some specific goal they set for themselves. For some the goal may be amassing[1] a million dollars, for others losing those annoying ten-plus pounds, and for still others it is finding a soulmate[2]. It could be getting a better job, driving a nicer car, or pursuing a dream career. Whatever your " there" is, you may be convinced that once you arrive, you will finally find the peace you have always dreamed of; you will finally become fulfilled, happy, and content.

However, more often than not, once you arrive "there" you will still feel dissatisfied, and move your "there" vision to yet another point in the future. By always chasing after another "there," you are never really appreciating what you already have right "here." It is important for human beings to keep "sober-minded[3]" about the age-old drive to look beyond the place where you now stand. On one hand, your life is enhanced by your dreams and aspirations. On the other hand, these drives can pull you farther and farther from your enjoyment of your life right now.

People from the beginning of time have struggled with the question of how we can live in the present moment. And it is a challenge that has become particularly difficult in the modern world in which we are constantly lured[4] by visions of greater glory, beauty, fame. If you learn to be grateful, you can fulfill the challenge of living in the present.

To be grateful means you are thankful for and appreciative of

许多人都相信，一旦他们达到了自己所设定的某个特定目标，他们就会开心、快乐。这个目标因人而异，有人想要积聚万贯家产，有人想要减掉那讨厌的十几磅肉，也有人想要找到自己的心灵伴侣。这目标可以是更好的工作，更豪华的车子，或是理想的职业。不论你的"彼岸"是什么，有一点你是深信不疑的：只要你达到了，你就能最终找到你梦寐以求的安宁和平静；你也终将变得称心如意、快乐知足。

然而事实并非如此。在大多数情况下，当你到达彼岸时，你还是不知足、不满意，而且又有了新的彼岸——新的幻想和憧憬。由于你总是疲于追逐一个又一个的彼岸，你从未真正欣赏、珍惜你已经拥有的一切。不安于现状的欲望人皆有之，由来已久，但重要的是要对它保持清醒的头脑。一方面，你的生活因为梦想和渴望而更加精彩。另一方面，这些欲望又使你越来越不懂得珍惜和享受现在拥有的生活。

从远古时代开始人们就一直在苦苦思索这个问题——我们怎样才能生活在现实中。而到了现代社会里，这成了一个十分严峻的挑战，因为我们一刻不停地被各种各样的幻想、憧憬所诱惑——更多的荣耀、美貌、名

❶ amass
/əˈmæs/
vt. 积聚

❷ soulmate
/ˈsəulmeɪt/
n. 心灵伴侣

❸ sober-minded
adj. 头脑清醒的

❹ lure
/luə/
vt. 吸引，诱惑

what you have and where you are on your path right now. Gratitude fills your heart with the joyful feeling and allows you to fully appreciate everything that arises on your path. As you strive to keep your focus on the present moment, you can experience the full wonder of "here." There are many ways to cultivate[5] gratitude. Here are just a few suggestions you may wish to try:

Imagine what your life would be like if you lost all that you had. This will most surely remind you of how much you do appreciate it.

Make a list each day of all that you are grateful for, so that you can stay conscious daily of your blessings. Do this especially when you are feeling as though you have nothing to feel grateful for. Or spend a few minutes before you go to sleep giving thanks for all that you have.

Spend time offering assistance to those who are less fortunate than you, so that you may gain perspective[6].

However you choose to learn gratitude is irrelevant[7]. What really matters is that you create a space in your consciousness[8] for appreciation for all that you have right now, so that you may live more joyously in your present moment.

声和财富。假如你能懂得感恩，你就能真正生活在现实中。

感恩是指你感激、珍惜自己当前所拥有的一切以及所处的人生境遇。心存感恩，你的心灵就会充满愉悦，你就能真正领会人生路上的种种体验。如果你努力把眼光锁定在此时此刻，你就能感受它的美妙之处。感恩之心需要经常加强。许多方法可以培育感恩之心，你不妨试试以下几种：

1. 设想如果你失去了现在拥有的一切，你的生活将会怎么样。它肯定会使你意识到原来你是多么喜欢和珍视这一切。

2. 每天都列出那些值得你感激的事物，那样你就能时时刻刻意识到自己的幸运。每天都要这么做，尤其是当你觉得好像没有什么可感激的时候。另外你也可以每天临睡前花几分钟感激自己拥有的一切。

3. 花时间帮助那些没有你那么幸运的人，这样你也许会对生活有正确的认识。

其实，你选择何种方法去学会感恩无关紧要，真正重要的是你应该有意识地努力去欣赏和珍视你现在所拥有的一切，这样你就可以更快乐地享受你目前的生活。

❺ **cultivate**
/ˈkʌltɪveɪt/
v.培养

❻ **perspective**
/pəˈspektɪv/
n. 正确观察事物的能力，眼力

❼ **irrelevant**
/ɪˈreləvənt/
adj.不相关的

❽ **consciousness**
/ˈkɒnʃəsnɪs/
n.意识

Two frogs
两只青蛙

It is sometimes hard to understand that an encouraging word can go such a long way.

有时,很难相信一个鼓励的字眼竟能起到如此大的作用!

A group of frogs were traveling through the woods, and two of them fell into a deep pit. When they saw how deep the pit was, they told the two frogs that they were as good as dead. The two frogs ignored the comments and tried to jump up out of the pit with all their might[1]. The other frogs kept telling them to stop, that they were as good as dead. Finally, one of the frogs took heed[2] of what the other frogs were saying and gave up. He fell down and died. The other frog continued to jump as hard as he could. Once again, the crowd of frogs yelled[3] at him to stop the pain and just die. He jumped even harder and finally made it out. When he got out, the other frogs said, "Did you not hear us?" The frog explained to them that he was deaf. He thought they were encouraging him the entire time.

This story teaches us two lessons:

1. There is power of life and death in the tongue[4]. An encouraging word to someone who is down can lift them up and help them make it through the day.

2. A destructive[5] word to someone who is down can be what it takes to kill them.

Be careful of what you say. Speak life to those who cross your path. The power of words...it is sometimes hard to understand that an encouraging word can go such a long way. Anyone can speak words that tend to rob another of the spirit to continue in difficult times. Special is the individual[6] who will take the time to encourage another.

一群青蛙在穿越树林时，其中两只失足落入一个深坑。大家看到这个坑的深度时就对这两只青蛙说，他们只有死路一条了。但这两只青蛙全不理会同伴们的话，相反，他们使出全力以图跳出这深坑。青蛙们仍不停地奉劝他们算了，并坚持说他俩只有死路一条。最后，其中一只青蛙听从了大家的劝告，放弃了。于是，他掉下去死了；而另一只青蛙却还竭尽全力地跳着。众青蛙又一次向他大声提醒，奉劝他别再自讨苦吃了，安息吧！谁知，他跳得更加卖力，终于他跳了出来！当他出来之后，大伙问他："你没听到我们的话吗？"这只青蛙解释说，他是个聋子，他还以为大家一直是在鼓励他呢！

这则故事有两个寓意：

1.福祸皆从口出，话语有决定人死生的力量。一句鼓励的话能使情绪低落的人重新振作，帮助他们走出困境。

2.一句伤人的话能要了一个情绪低落的人的性命。

人们一定要思其所言！向每天经过你左右的人说积极向上的话。不可小看言语的力量……有时，很难相信一个鼓励的字眼竟能起到如此大的作用！任何人都能说出夺去他人战胜困境的勇气和意志的话，而只有愿意花时间去鼓励别人的人才是最特别、最值得尊重的。

❶ **might**
/maɪt/
n.力量，能力
with all one's might
竭尽全力
❷ **heed**
/hiːd/
v.注意
❸ **yell**
/jel/
v.号叫；呼喊
❹ **tongue**
/tʌŋ/
n.舌；舌头
❺ **destructive**
/dɪˈstrʌktɪv/
adj.毁灭性的
❻ **individual**
/ˌɪndɪˈvɪdʒuəl/
n.（口）人

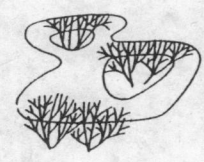

Others are only mirrors of you
别人其实是你的一面镜子

Your judgment of someone will not serve as a protective shield against you becoming like him.

你对别人做出的评论,并不是可以保证你不会像他那样的盾牌。

The first time you meet someone, in the first moment you form an impression in your mind of that person. Your reactions to other people, however, are really just barometers[1] for how you perceive yourself. Your reactions to others say more about you than they do about others. You cannot really love or hate something about another person unless it reflects something you love or hate about yourself. We are usually drawn to those who are most like us and tend to dislike those who display those aspects of ourselves that we dislike.

Therefore, you can allow others to be the mirror to illuminate[2] more clearly your own feelings of self-worth. Conversely, you can view the people you judge negatively as mirrors to show you what you are not accepting about yourself.

To coexist peacefully with others, you will need to learn tolerance. A big challenge is to shift your perspective radically from judgment of other to a lifelong exploration of yourself. Your task is to assess all the decisions, judgments you make onto others and to begin to view them as clues to how you can heal yourself and become whole.

I recently had a business lunch with a man who displayed objectionable[3] table manners. My first reaction was to judge him as offensive and his table manners as disgusting. When I noticed that I was judging him, I stopped and asked myself what I was feeling. I discovered that I was embarrassed to be seen with someone who was chewing with his mouth open and loudly blow-

当你与某人初次见面时，你首先会在脑子里对他形成一个印象。然而，你对别人的反应其实正反映了你对自己的看法。这与其说是对别人的评判，倒不如说是对你的自我评判。你不会真的那么喜欢或讨厌别人的某个方面，除非这也是你自身所存在的某个优点或缺点。物以类聚，人以群分，我们总是喜欢那些与自己最相像的人，而讨厌另一些人，因为他们有着我们自身所存在的某些缺点。

这样一来，你能够以他人为鉴，更清楚地反映自己对自我价值的感受。相反，你也能以那些你不认同的人为鉴，由此了解你对自己所不认同的方面。

为了与他人和平共处，你要学会宽容。一个巨大的挑战就是彻底转变你的视角：不去评判别人，而要永远探查自我。你的任务就是审视你对别人所做的评定和判断，并以此为契机来改进、完善自我。

最近，我与一个客户共进工作午餐，他的餐桌礼仪实在让人不敢恭维。我的第一反应就判定他是个不懂规矩的家伙，就餐没有礼貌，令人生厌。当我意识到自己正在评论他时，我停下来问自己是什么感受。我发现，原来我非常害怕被人看到跟这么一个张着嘴

❶ **barometer**
/bəˈrɒmɪtə/
n. 晴雨表；能显示变化的事物
❷ **illuminate**
/ɪˈluːmɪneɪt/
vt. 照亮，照明
❸ **objectionable**
/əbˈdʒekʃnəbl/
adj. 令人不快的，不适合的

ing his nose. I was astonished[4] to find how much I cared about how the other people in the restaurant perceived[5] me.

Remember that your judgment of someone will not serve as a protective shield[6] against you becoming like him. Just because I judged my lunch partner as offensive[7] does not prevent me from ever looking or acting like him. In the same way, extending tolerance to him would not cause me to suddenly begin chewing my food with my mouth open.

When you approach life in this manner, those with whom you have the greatest grievances[8] as well as those you admire and love can be seen as mirrors, guiding you to discover parts of yourself that you reject and to embrace your greatest qualities.

咀嚼、大声地擤鼻涕的人在一起，这让我很尴尬。我非常惊讶自己原来如此在乎餐馆里的其他人对我的看法。

记住，你对别人做出的评论，并不是可以保证你不会像他那样的盾牌。比如，我把我那位一起就餐的客户判定为不懂规矩的家伙，但这并不能保证我永远都不会有他那样的行为。同样，如果我对他宽容，这并不会使我突然也张着嘴咀嚼。

如果你这样看待生活，你就能以人为镜，即使是你最不满的人也可以与你所尊敬和喜爱的人一样成为你的镜子，引导你发现对自己不认同的地方、更好地认同自己的优点。

❹ **astonish**
/əˈstɒnɪʃ/
v. 使大为惊异
❺ **perceive**
/pəˈsiːv/
v. 感觉
❻ **shield**
/ʃiːld/
n. 盾
❼ **offensive**
/əˈfensiv/
adj. 令人不快的
❽ **grievance**
/ˈgriːvns/
n. 不满

No scorecard[1] in marriage
婚姻生活中不需要记分卡

In a marriage, there are some things you like to do and some things you don't.

在婚姻生活中，总有些事情是你喜欢做的，有些是你不喜欢做的。

When I came home for the holidays my sophomore'[2] year of college, I thought I knew everything. I was on the big female independence kick. One evening, my mom and I were wrapping presents, and I told her that when I got married, my husband was going to help clean, do laundry[3], cook, the whole bit. Then I asked her if she ever got tired of doing the laundry and dishes. She calmly told me it did not bother her. This was difficult for me to believe. I began to <u>give her a lecture</u>[4] about this being the '90s, and equality between the sexes.

Mom listened patiently. Then after setting the ribbon[5] aside, she looked me square in the eyes.

"Someday, dear, you will understand."

This only irritated[6] me more. I didn't understand one bit. And so I demanded more of an explanation. Mom smiled and began to explain:

"In a marriage, there are some things you like to do and some things you don't. So, together, you figure out what little things you are willing to do for each other. You share the responsibilities. I really don't mind doing the laundry. Sure, it takes some time, but it is something I do for your dad. On the other hand, I do not like to pump[7] gas. The smell of the fumes bothers me. And I don't like to stand out in the freezing cold. So, your dad always puts gas in my car. Your dad grocery shops, and I cook. Your dad mows[8] the grass, and I clean. I could go on and on."

婚姻生活中不需要记分卡

我大学二年级那年回家度假的时候，我自认为已经无所不知了，尤其是对于男女不平等的现象可谓是深恶痛绝。有天晚上我和妈妈正在包裹礼物，我对妈妈说，将来我结婚以后，我一定要让我的丈夫帮着做家务，什么打扫卫生啦、洗熨衣物啦、做饭啦，等等。接着，我问妈妈是否对整日洗熨衣物、刷锅洗碗感到厌倦，她却平静地对我说她从来都没有感到厌烦。这简直让我难以置信。于是，我开始向她大谈特谈什么如今已是20世纪90年代了，什么两性平等啦等等。

妈妈耐心地听着我高谈阔论。在礼物的包裹上系上丝带，然后她注视着我的眼睛说："亲爱的，将来你会明白的。"

这不禁令我非常生气。我一点儿也不明白！于是，我要求妈妈为我做进一步解释。妈妈笑着解释道：

"在婚姻生活中，总有些事情是你喜欢做的，有些是你不喜欢做的。因此，夫妻二人一定要互相交流，看看有哪些事情是你愿意为对方做的。此外，夫妻二人要共同分担责任。我真的从来都没有在意过洗熨衣物等家务事。当然，做这些琐事确实花了我不少时间，但是，这是为你爸爸做的。相反，我不喜欢去给汽车加油，那种难闻的味道着实让

---

❶ scorecard
/ˈskɔːkɑːd/
n. 记分卡

❷ sophomore
/ˈsɒfəmɔː/
n. (美) 大学二年级学生

❸ laundry
/ˈlɔːndrɪ/
n. 洗衣店

❹ give sb. a lecture
教训某人，向某人说教

❺ ribbon
/ˈrɪbən/
n. 狭长带子

❻ irritate
/ˈɪrɪteɪt/
v. 激怒

❼ pump
/pʌmp/
v. 打气

❽ mow
/məʊ/
v. 割

"You see," my mother continued, "in marriage, there is no scorecard. You do little things for each other to make the other's life easier. If you think of it as helping the person you love, you don't become annoyed[9] with doing the laundry or cooking, or any task, because you're doing it out of love."

Over the years, I have often reflected on what my mom said. She has a great perspective on marriage. I like how my mom and dad take care of each other. And you know what? One day, when I'm married, I don't want to have a scorecard either.

我难以承受，而且我也不喜欢站在寒冷的车外等着加油。所以，总是你爸爸去为我的汽车加油。还有，你爸爸负责到杂货店买东西，我负责做饭；你爸爸负责割草；而我就负责清理。当然，还有很多这样的事。"

"你知道吗？"妈妈继续语重心长地说，"在婚姻生活中，是不需要计分卡的。夫妻二人各自为对方做了一些力所能及的事可以让彼此的生活更加舒适，更加从容。只要你想到这是帮你的爱人做的，你就不会再在意这些洗熨衣物、烧菜做饭等等的家务事，或是其他的一些事情。因为你这么做完全是因为爱啊！"

这么多年来，我一直都在思考着妈妈说过的那些话。关于婚姻生活，她的观点确实非常有意义。我喜欢妈妈和爸爸的这种互相关怀，互相照顾的方式。你知道吗，将来我结婚以后，我也不想在夫妻之间有计分卡。

❾ annoy
/əˈnɔɪ/
v. 打搅；烦忧

All about love
关 于 恋 情

I love you not because of who you are, but because of who I am when I am with you.

我爱你不是因为你了不起，而是因为与你在一起时我自己的那种感觉。

I love you not because of who you are, but because of who I am when I am with you.

No man or woman is worth your tears, and the one who is, won't make you cry.

Just because someone doesn't love you the way you want them to, doesn't mean they don't love you with all they have.

A true friend is someone who reaches for your hand and touches your heart.

The worst way to miss someone is to be sitting right beside them knowing you can't have them.

Never frown[1], even when you are sad, because you never know who is falling in love with your smile.

To the world you may be one person, but to one person you may be the world.

Don't waste time on a man/ woman, who isn't willing to waste their time on you.

Maybe God wants us to meet a few wrong people before meeting the right one, so that when we finally meet the person, we will know how to be grateful.

关于恋情

我爱你不是因为你了不起,而是因为与你在一起时我自己的那种感觉。

他或她不值得你黯然神伤,因为一个值得你为之落泪的人是不会让你流泪伤心的。

他或许没有按你希望的方式在爱着你,但这并不说明这份爱不是全心全意的。

真正的朋友不仅能握住你的双手,而且能触及你的心灵。

思念一个人最痛苦的情形是:你与此人近在咫尺,却无法将其拥有。

永远不要皱眉,即使你很悲伤,因为你不知道谁会倾心你的淡淡一笑。

对全世界来说你或许只是千万人中的一个,但对某个人来说你却会是整个世界。

不要把时间浪费在某个人身上,如果此人不愿在你身上花费时间。

相识无缘人多少,难遇有缘人一个,有朝一日遇此人,方有万分感谢。这或许是上帝的有意安排。

不要为感情结束而难过,只要有过,就该微笑。

感情难免受到伤害,但不能因此不再信任他人;只是下次信任时要多加小心。

追求和了解一位新朋友,并希望人家了解你,先要完善自己,认识自己。

❶ frown
/fraʊn/
v. 皱眉

Don't cry because it is over; smile because it happened.

There's always going to people that hurt you so what you have to do is keep on trusting and just be more careful about who you trust next time around.

Make yourself a better person and know who you are before you try and know someone else and expect them to know you.

Don't try so hard, for the best things come when you least expect them to.

Remember: whatever happens happens for a reason.

凡事不要强求,期待值越低,结果却可能越好。

记住:任何事情发生都有其理由。

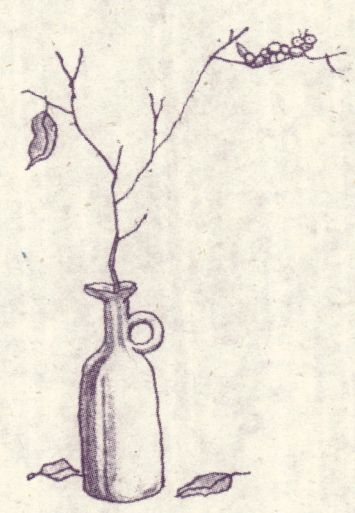

Relax
休息放松

The important thing is to manage stress and anxiety so that it doesn't affect your emotional and physical health.

化解压力和焦虑是重要的,如此才不会影响身心健康。

Some people are always on the go[1], full of worry and tension. These people don't take time to relax, and more often than not, respond to daily anxiety and stress by tensing their muscles. This causes muscle fatigue and may result in loss of muscle tone, and a general deterioration[2] in outward appearance.

Consider someone you know who appears to have "the weight of the world" on his/her shoulders. Chances are, this person looks 5 to 10 years older than he/she really is due to worry and stress, which can weaken the immune system and increase vulnerability[3] to diseases and other health problems. Learning how to relax in the face of today's anxiety, tension and stress can be an important step in slowing the aging process.

There are a number of methods to help you relax, including deep breathing, meditation[4], visualization[5] and, believe it or not, exercise. One of the most popular and successful relaxation techniques involves tensing and relaxing individual muscle groups. This technique can be used while lying in bed or sitting in a comfortable chair. Start at your feet, tensing and then relaxing your toes for ten seconds at a time. Then progress upward to the calf[6] muscles, thigh muscles, shoulder and neck muscles, and finish up with your facial muscles. After a few days of progressive muscle relaxation, you'll begin to recognize tense muscle areas and begin to relax them.

The important thing is to manage stress and anxiety so that it doesn't affect your emotional and physical health. By learning how

有些人总是忙个不停，紧张不已，烦恼不断。他们不花时间来休息放松，面对每天的焦虑与压力多半是愁眉苦脸。这会引起肌肉疲劳，还可能导致肌肉失去弹性，整个外表全然失色。

留心一下似乎"重任"在肩的某个熟人。由于烦恼和压力，他或她很可能看起来要比实际年龄老5到10岁。烦恼和压力会削弱人的免疫系统，增加疾病和其他健康问题的易发性。面对现今社会中的焦虑、紧张和压力，学会如何放松可能是延缓衰老的重要途径。

有些方法可以帮助你放松，包括深呼吸、冥想、想象，还有——信不信由你——锻炼。其中最流行和最有效的放松技巧之一是绷紧和松弛个别的肌群。这种方法不管是躺在床上还是坐在安乐椅上均可用。先从脚趾做起，每次绷紧再松弛脚趾10秒钟。接着向上转到腿肚肌、大腿肌、肩、脖肌，一直做到脸部肌肉为止。经过几天循序渐进的肌肉放松后，你就会开始察觉绷紧的肌肉区，并开始使它们松弛。

化解压力和焦虑是重要的，如此才不会影响身心健康。学会如何放松，便能甩掉肩上的沉重包袱，把精力集中于积极的生活方

❶ on the go
忙碌的
❷ deterioration
/dɪˌtɪərɪəˈreɪʃn/
n. 变坏的，变质
❸ vulnerability
/ˌvʌlnərəˈbɪlɪtɪ/
n. 脆弱性，容易受伤害性
❹ meditation
/ˌmedɪˈteɪʃn/
n. 冥想
❺ visualization
/ˌvɪʒʊəlaɪˈzeɪʃn/
n. 想象
❻ calf
/kɑːf/
n. 小腿

to relax, you can remove the weight of the world from your shoulders and focus on the positive aspects[7] of life. You'll slow the aging process and look years younger.

面。这样就可延缓衰老进程,使你看起来年轻许多。

7 aspect
/'æspekt/
n.特殊部分

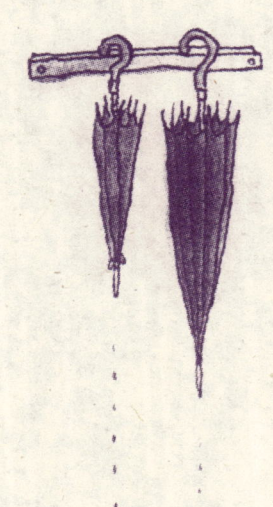

What you make of your life is up to you
生活全由你自己去创造

In this world, we have countless people who have proven that a person can do whatever he or she strives to do.

在这个世界上,人们一次又一次地证实了这么一个道理:世上无难事,只怕有心人。

Every person creates his or her own reality. Authorship of your life is one of your absolute rights; yet so often people deny that they have the ability to script[1] the life they desire. They <u>look past</u>[2] the fundamental truth that it is not our external resources that determine our success or failure, but rather our own belief in ourselves and our willingness to create a life according to our highest aspirations.

Clearly, the challenge here is to create and own your own reality. When you begin to live your life understanding that what you make of it is up to you, you are able to design it according to your authentic choices and desires. You will learn lessons here, such as responsibility and limitlessness, which will lead you to the life you were meant to live. These lessons provide you with the essential tools you need in order to take command of your life

Responsibility To take responsibility means you admit your accountability[3] and acknowledge your influence and role in the circumstances in which you find yourself. It means you <u>are answerable for</u>[4] your behavior and you fully accept any consequences created by your actions.

To take responsibility will propel[5] you forward and onward to your greater goal. I know of a woman named Mary whose story of personal responsibility has always inspired me. Mary was born in Cuba and moved to Miami with her family when she was two years old. They lived in terrible poverty in a dangerous part of the city, where crime and drugs were part of everyday life. Mary was

生活全由你自己去创造

每个人的生活都是由他或她自己创造的。每个人都绝对享有创造自己生活的权利,然而人们总是否认他们有能力描绘自己所向往的人生。他们忽视了一个根本的事实,即决定我们成功与失败的不是外在条件,而在于我们对自己有没有信心,是否愿意根据自己的最高志向创造生活。

显然,这里的挑战是创造并掌握自己的生活。你一旦明白自己是生活的创造者并开始努力创造生活,你就能够按照自己真正的选择与愿望去设计人生。在这里你将学到的课程是承担责任和潜能无限,它们将带你走进你想要的生活,并将给予你主宰自己的生活所必需的重要手段。

承担责任 承担责任是指你认同自己负有责任,承认自己在自身所处环境中的影响和作用。也就是说你为自己的行为负责,完全承担由自己的行为所造成的一切后果。

承担责任能推动你不断前进,创造更美好的前程。我知道一个叫玛丽的女人,她那勇于对自己负责的事迹一直让我备受鼓舞。玛丽出生在古巴,两岁时举家搬迁到迈阿密市。他们的生活极度贫困,所住的地方是迈阿密的危险地区,犯罪和毒品肆虐成灾。然而,小小年纪的玛丽在她8岁时就立志要干出

❶ script
/skrɪpt/
vt. 书写,(喻)创造
❷ look past
忽视
❸ accountability
/əˌkaʊntəˈbɪlɪtɪ/
n. 责任,负责
❹ be answerable for=be responsible for
应负责的
❺ propel
/prəˈpel/
vt. 推动,推进

determined, however, even at the young age of eight, to make something of her life other than follow the expected route of becoming a maid, or a cashier at the local supermarket. So she got herself to school each and every, day, sometimes having to step over drunks <u>passed out</u>[6] in the doorway, just so she could get education and give herself a better life.

Mary eventually left Miami, obtained a good education, and fostered[7] her natural music ability. Mary could have given in to the life she was born into, or remained mired[8] in blaming her parents and culture for her circumstances. She could have refused to take responsibility for the situation. Instead, however, Mary took responsibility for herself and created a life of which she can be proud.

Responsibility is a major lesson of adulthood. If you still haven't learned the lesson of responsibility, it's not too late. Remember, life will provide you with plenty of opportunities to get it right.

Limitlessness Limitlessness is the sense that there are no boundaries to what you can become or do. You learn it when you know that your evolution is never-ending and your potential for growth reaches to infinity[9].

You were born knowing your limitlessness. As you grew and became socialized in this world, however, you might have come to believe that there are boundaries that prevent you from reach-

一番事业，而不是走她本该走的生活道路——当个女佣或是当地超市的收银员。为此，她每天准时上学，从不旷课，有时甚至不得不从那些醉倒在家门口的酒鬼身上跨过去，因为只有这样她才能受到教育，为自己创造更好的生活。

玛丽最终离开了迈阿密，获得了良好的教育，并发展了她的音乐天赋。玛丽本来可以屈服于她与生俱来的命运，或者一直深陷于埋怨自己的父母与所属的文化之中。对此她完全可以拒绝承担任何责任。然而，她为自己承担了责任，并且创造了值得自己骄傲的生活。

承担责任是每个成年人的一门主修课。如果你还没有学会承担责任这门课，现在还为时不晚。记住，生活会给你提供许许多多的机会去学会承担责任.

潜能无限 潜能无限，即没有任何东西可以限制你成为你想成为的人，做到你想做到的事。如果你相信自己的进步是永无止境的，自己的发展潜力是无穷无尽的，那你就学会了这一课。

刚来到世上时，你就知道自己的潜能是无限的，然而，随着你在这个世界上慢慢地成长，逐渐融入社会生活，你可能就开始相

❻ **pass out**
昏过去；失去知觉
❼ **foster**
/ˈfɒstə/
vt. 培养，发展
❽ **mire**
/ˈmaɪə/
v. 使陷入困境
❾ **infinity**
/ɪnˈfɪnɪtɪ/
n. 无穷无尽，无极限

ing the highest levels of spiritual, emotional, or mental evolution. However, boundaries exist only in your mind. When you are able to transcend[10] them, you learn the lesson of limitlessness.

When I was young, I had a teacher who understood the importance of this lesson. She reminded us every day that we could do anything we set our minds to, no matter how impossible it might seem or how strong the opposition is. It is my sincere hope that there is a teacher like Mrs. Carbone in every school around the world, so that our children can know the wonder and power they have within themselves and will strive to access it.

In this world, we have countless people who have proven that a person can do whatever he or she strives to do.

信有种种极限妨碍你，使你不能达到精神、情感和思想上的最高层次。然而，这些极限只存在于你的心里。如果你能超越这些极限，那你就学到了潜能无限这一课。

我小时候的一位老师(卡蓬夫人)深信这一课程的重要性。她天天提醒我们：只要下定决心，我们就能做好每一件事，不管是看起来根本不可能的事，还是受到重重阻挠的事。我真诚地希望世界上的每所学校都有像卡蓬夫人这样的老师，这样，我们的孩子就会懂得他们身上拥有惊人的才能和力量，而且会努力向前奋进。

在这个世界上，人们一次又一次地证实了这么一个道理：世上无难事，只怕有心人。

⑩ **transcend**
/trænˈsend/
vt. 超越

Food for thought
精神食粮

Love begins with a smile, grows with a kiss and ends with a tear.

爱始于微笑，育于亲吻，调于泪水。

are moments in life when you miss someone so much that you just want to pick them from your dreams and hug them for real!

When the door of happiness closes, another opens, but often times we look so long at the closed door that we don't see the one which has been opened for us.

Don't go for looks; they can deceive[1]. Don't go for wealth; even that fades away. Go for someone who makes you smile because it takes only a smile to make a dark day seem bright. Find the one that makes your heart smile.

Dream what you want to dream; go where you want to go; be what you want to be, because you have only one life and one chance to do all the things you want to do.

May you have enough happiness to make you sweet, enough trials to make you strong, enough sorrow to keep you human, enough hope to make you happy.

The happiest of people don't necessarily have the best of everything; they just make the most of everything that comes along their way.

Love begins with a smile, grows with a kiss and ends with a tear.

生命中有这样的时刻，我们对一个人朝思暮想，只想一把把她从梦中拉出来，拥她入怀！

一扇通往幸福的门关闭了，另一扇通往幸福的门会打开。可有多少次啊，我们徘徊在那扇关闭的门前，却忽略了那扇早已为我们开启的新的幸福之门。

不要以貌取人，花容月貌也许会欺骗你的双眸；不要追逐钱财，钱财会消失枯竭；去寻找那个会让你笑口常开的人吧，因为一个微笑就可以使我们郁闷的日子云开雾散，风和日丽。去努力找寻那个令你心灵愉悦的人吧！

做你想做的梦，去你想去的地方，走你想走的路吧！因为生命只有一次，我们仅有一次机会来做我们想做的事情。

愿你与幸福永伴，使你亲切可爱；愿你历经磨难，使你坚韧不拔；愿你痛彻心肺，使你懂得同情；愿你满怀希望，使你天天快乐。

世界上最幸福的人并不一定拥有一切最好的东西，他们只是最充分利用、珍惜了他们生命中的一切。

爱始于微笑，育于亲吻，凋于流泪。

最美好的未来扎根于我们对过去的遗忘，

❶ deceive
/dɪˈsiːv/
v. 欺骗

The brightest future will always be based on a forgotten past, you can't go on well in life until you let go of your past failures and heartaches.

When you were born, you were crying and everyone around you was smiling. Live your life so that when you die, you're the one who is smiling and everyone around you is crying.

只有对曾经的失败与挫折不再耿耿于怀，生命才会变得更加美好。

乍临人世，你在哭，周围的人在笑；要认真地生活，临别人世，你在笑，周围的人却在哭。

Support
支持

She realized that her own tears required as much attention and nurturing from her as anyone else's.

她认识到自己的眼泪与别人的一样，也需要得到她的关心和爱护。

"There are two ways of spreading light: to be the candle or the mirror that reflect it."

—— Wharton

You support someone when you willingly step forward to help him through a challenging time. Yet the great irony¹ is that when you support others, you are also, in fact, supporting yourself. When you withhold² support from others, it is usually an indicator that you are also withholding support from yourself.

We are most often called upon to support others in friendship. One of my acquaintances, Donna, told me a story recently that clearly illustrates the magic of support and its potential as an emotional mirror.

Several years ago, Donna had been feeling very depressed. She had just broken up with her boyfriend of two years, and she was having a very difficult time accepting the loss. She had <u>been laid up</u>³ with a knee injury for several days, and the time alone at home certainly was not helping. Her misery was only compounded by her frustration at herself for not being able to pull it together and stop crying all the time.

Early one morning, Donna received a phone call with some terrible news: her best friend's brother had been killed in a car accident. Donna had known this friend, Mary, and her brother nearly her entire life, and the news was devastating⁴. However, Donna quickly pulled herself together, got in the car, and drove to

支 持

"传播光明的方法有两种：要么做一根蜡烛，要么做一面镜子去反射蜡烛的光明。"

——沃顿

如果你能自愿上前帮助他人度过难关，你这就是在支持他。但是也许你没有想到，当你在支持他人时，你其实就是在支持自己。相反，如果你拒绝给予他人支持，这通常表明你也在拒绝自己。

朋友之间最需要相互支持。最近，我的一位熟人唐娜向我讲述了一个故事，这正好清楚地阐述了支持的神奇魔力以及它作为情感上的镜子的巨大潜力。

几年前，唐娜曾一度萎靡不振，因为她与交往了两年的男友刚刚分手，非常难以接受这种失去的现实。接着她又因为膝盖受伤卧床数天。这样独自在家的日子，肯定是难挨的。她为自己未能自控、成天哭个不停而沮丧、懊恼，这又加剧了她的痛苦。

一天清晨，唐娜接到一个电话，得知了一个噩耗：她最要好的朋友的弟弟在车祸中丧生。唐娜和这位朋友玛丽和她的弟弟有着多年的交情，可以算是一辈子的朋友，这一消息令唐娜悲痛万分。但是她很快控制住自己，立刻开车赶到了玛丽家里陪伴她。

在以后的几天里，在忙着张罗葬礼、接

❶ irony
/ˈaɪərəni/
n. 嘲弄，讽刺

❷ withhold
/wɪðˈhəʊld/
vt. 拒绝

❸ be laid up
因病卧床

❹ devastating
/ˈdevəsteɪtɪŋ/
adj. 毁灭性的

her friend's house to be there with her.

Over the course of the next few days, amidst the haze[5] of the funeral and hundreds of visitors, Donna was 100 percent present for Mary. She held her close while she cried endless tears, sat by her side as the waves of grief washed over her friend, and slept on the floor next to Mary's bed to make sure she did not wake up alone in the middle of the night. During that time she hardly felt any pain in her knee at all and none of the depression she had been experiencing.

Several weeks later, when life began to return to normal, Donna realized that the level of support she had given Mary far exceeded any support she had offered herself during her dark time. She was able to use the support she had given her friend as a mirror for the support she had been withholding from herself. She realized that her own tears required as much attention and nurturing from her as anyone else's, and that if she could give it to another, she must be able to also give it to herself..

So, when you find yourself unable to support someone else, look within and see if perhaps there is something within yourself that you are not supporting. Conversely, when you give complete support to others, it will mirror those places within you that require the same level of attention.

待众多吊唁者的同时，唐娜一刻不离地陪在玛丽的身边。当玛丽失声痛哭不能自已时，唐娜紧紧地搂着她；当玛丽悲伤过度，痛不欲生时，唐娜紧伴其左右；夜晚，为了让玛丽不会在黑夜里独自惊醒，唐娜就睡在玛丽床边的地板上。在那段时间里，唐娜几乎忘了她膝盖的伤痛以及自己曾经经历的消沉。

几星期后，生活恢复了正常。这时，唐娜意识到自己给予了玛丽极大的支持，却根本未曾在自己失意的时候给予自己以同样的支持。给朋友的支持犹如一面镜子，使唐娜认识到自己曾经吝于支持自我。她认识到自己的眼泪与别人的一样，也需要得到她的关心和爱护；而且如果她可以关心、爱护别人，她也必定能够关心、爱护自己。

所以，当你发现自己吝于给予他人支持、安慰时，你应该扪心自问，看看自己是否有某些被拒绝支持的地方。反过来，如果你能够不遗余力地去支持他人，你也会因此发现自己也有某些值得同样关心、爱护的脆弱之处。

❺ haze
/heɪz/
n. 心中的迷惑

On the shoulders of a hero
坐在勇士的肩膀上

All that time, it turned out, he had been there — sharing my life.

事实证明,每时每刻,他都一直在我的身边——分享我的人生。

My father went into intensive care, his heart not working right. As word went out, each of his six grown children sped toward Venice Hospital in Florida, where he lay attached to various machines. Late that night, we stood around him with our mother, holding his hands and speaking close to his face as he strained against some powerful force that kept on pulling him away.

"Good-bye, Dad," we said. "We love you. Thank you, Dad. Oh, no ..."

A breath left his body under our hands, and we turned to watch the numbers on the machines. Then we made an involuntary[1], collective groan, and he was gone. He was 75 years old.

With his passing, I was abruptly stripped of [2] any illusions about my own immortality; no longer might I comfort myself with the thought that he was in line ahead of me. I was newly alone and vulnerable and, more than ever, responsible for my life.

Then I remembered one morning when I was five years old. After a snowstorm, Dad carried me on his shoulders for the mile from our apartment into town. As he marched bravely through the snowdrifts, I put my hands around his head to hold on, inadvertently[3] covering his eyes with my mittens. "I can't see," my father said, but he walked on nevertheless, a blind hero making his way with me on his back through a strange, magical landscape of untrodden[4] snow. He had returned recently from World War II, and this ride would become my first experience with him to take hold

父亲开始接受重症病人的加护治疗，他的心脏不正常了。6个已长大成人的儿女得知这个消息后，马不停蹄地赶到佛罗里达的维尼斯医院。父亲正躺在病床上，身边是各种各样的急救医疗仪器。夜已经很深了，我们和母亲一起围在他的床前，紧握住他的手，贴近他的脸和他说话。当时仿佛有某种强大的力量要把他带走，而他正竭力挣扎抗拒着。

"再见了，爸爸，"我们喃喃地对他说，"我们爱您。爸爸，谢谢您。噢，不……"

在我们紧握的手中，他咽下了最后一口气。我们转过身去看仪器上显示的数字，不禁失声痛哭起来。父亲就这样走了，享年75岁。

父亲的过世，让我突然意识到人生无常，自己的永生只不过是幻想；过去想到父亲在我面前走着，我就感到宽慰和踏实，现在却再也不可能了。我顿时变得孤独和脆弱，也比以前多了一份对我的生命的责任感。

我回想起一个早晨，那时我5岁。一场暴风雪过后，父亲把我驮在他的肩膀上，离家去一英里开外的城里。当他勇敢地迈过一个又一个雪堆时，我双手抱住他的头以坐稳些，手套却无意中遮住了他的眼睛。"我看不见了，"父亲说道，但他仍然继续前行。就这

❶ involuntary
/ɪnˈvɒləntərɪ/
adj. 不自觉的，无意识的

❷ strip sb. of sth.
剥夺；使某人失去某物

❸ inadvertently
/ˌɪnədˈvɜːtntlɪ/
adv. 无意地，非故意地

❹ un-trodden
adj. (trodden是tread的过去分词) 无人走过的

as a genuine[5], lasting memory.

As he was buried, other memories flooded in, and I found myself trying to put my feelings about him into perspective. How much of a father, really, had he been? Why hadn't I grieved more over losing him? Had I ever forgiven him for his shortcomings?

From my teenage years onward, I had expected a great deal of encouragement from my dad, but it seldom came. I told him, after senior year of high school, that I wanted to become an actor. He launched[6] into a speech about the instability[7] of such a career: "The odds are you'd wind up holding a tin[8] cup on the corner."

As the years went by, his expressions of doubt in response to my unspoken pleas for a father's blind faith became predictable. And I came to realize that my father's warnings were his way of relating to me. In earlier years I had thought he didn't care, but I came to understand that he was offering what he could.

I also realized that he had even inspired me — not by words, but by what he had done. He had come home from a terrifying war to raise six kids in a house with a yard. He had returned, with so many other men of his generation, to create stability and safety for those in his care and to give them a future.

He spent two decades in advertising and longer in real estate, meanwhile always taking us on vacations and sending us through college. By providing a foundation, he enabled his chil-

样，一位被蒙住眼睛的勇士背着我在无人走过的雪地里，在雪后陌生而神秘的景致里艰难跋涉。父亲当时刚从二战战场回来不久，这次旅行就成了我和他相处的第一次体验，是我最真的、永恒的回忆。

当他入土下葬的时候，其他的回忆如潮水般涌上心头，我发现自己正试图把对父亲的感情作出一个恰当的估计。作为一个父亲，他到底做得是否到位？为什么失去他我并没有悲痛欲绝？我宽恕了他的那些缺点吗？

从我十几岁时起，我就渴望父亲能给我很多鼓励，但他很少这样做。高中快毕业时，我告诉他我想成为一名演员。他马上就长篇大论，像发表演说一样，说这种职业有多么不稳定："结果你可能会拿着一个锡制的杯子，蜷缩在墙角乞讨。"

一年年过去了，对于我无言地要求一个父亲盲目的信任，父亲的怀疑成了预料中的事。但是我逐渐意识到父亲那些提醒正是他与我相处的一种方式。早些年我曾以为他对我漠不关心，但我现在慢慢明白，他已给了我他所能提供的一切。

我还意识到他实际上一直在激励着我——不是口头上，而是通过他的行动。他是经历了一场残酷恐怖的战争后回到家的，

❺ **genuine**
/ˈdʒenjʊɪn/
adj. 真正的；真实的

❻ **launch**
/lɔːntʃ/
v. 开始

❼ **instability**
/ˌɪnstəˈbɪlətɪ/
n. 不稳定

❽ **tin**
/tɪn/
n. 锡

dren to feel strong enough to go their individual ways. As we scattered, he wrote frequent letters and planned our reunion.

Just two weeks before he died, my father held a birthday celebration for Mom. We flew from our separate homes to Florida and, during our stay, joined him on a fishing trip. Dad did not look well.

We had no idea then how perilous[9] his condition had become. As I look back, it's clear that he had deliberately[10] kept all of that hidden from us to avoid spoiling our fun.

The moment we were to leave Florida, he pulled me aside and pointed to a mysterious box about three feet long and two feet deep. Inside, to my astonishment, were hundreds of clippings relating to almost everything I had done in my life. "I figured you might like to have this," Dad said.

We hugged each other, not knowing it would be for the last time, but my father must have sensed that he would not be around much longer.

Lifting the heavy box, I suddenly understood that no matter how negative his words had seemed, nothing could erase his concrete[11] act of filling the box, piece by piece, ever since I left home. All that time, it turned out, he had been there — sharing my life.

要在一栋有庭院的房子里抚养6个孩子。他和同时代的许多人一样，从战场上归来，要为那些需要他照料的人创造安稳的生活，要给他们一个未来。

他在广告业干了20年，在房地产业干的时间更长。与此同时，他还常常带我们出去度假，把我们一个个送去读大学。他为我们打好了基础，让我们感觉自己足够强壮，可以各奔前程。在我们天各一方以后，他经常给我们写信，安排一家人的团聚。

在他逝世前两个星期，父亲给母亲开了个生日庆祝会。我们从天南地北赶到佛罗里达，这期间还和父亲一起去钓了鱼。父亲的脸色看上去不是很好。

当时我们根本没想到父亲的病已到危险期。我回过头想一想，很明显父亲有意掩饰了这一切，他不愿意破坏这欢乐的气氛。

离开佛罗里达的那天早晨，父亲把我拉到一边，指给我看一个约有3英尺长、2英尺高的神秘的盒子。我打开一看，大吃一惊，里面装有几百张报纸的剪报，几乎涉及我有生以来做过的全部事情。"我想你可能会喜欢这些。"父亲说道。

我们紧紧拥抱，却不曾想到这竟会是诀别，但是父亲肯定已经意识到自己将不久于

⑨ perilous
/ˈperɪləs/
adj. 危险的
⑩ deliberately
/dɪˈlɪbərətlɪ/
adv. 故意地
⑪ concrete
/ˈkɒnkriːt/
adj. 具体存在的

Then came word that he was dying, and then came the months of thinking about him. Now a full year and a half have gone by without him, and I miss him beyond words. What I miss most, ironically, is that time long ago when I was a boy trusting his father to carry him blindly through life and to protect him. The security lay in simply knowing he was there.

人世了。

　　托起这沉甸甸的盒子,我突然明白了,无论父亲的话听上去有多么消极,什么都不能抹去那份实实在在的行动——自从我离家以后,他就一张一张地将纸条往盒子里装。事实证明,每时每刻,他都一直在我的身边——分享我的人生。

　　然后就得知父亲病危,接下来就是几个月的思念与缅怀。现在父亲过世已整整一年半了,我无法用言语来表达我对他的怀念之情。可笑的是,最让我难忘的是许多年前当我还是一个小孩子的时候,完全信任父亲蒙着眼睛带着我穿行人生,保护着我。我感觉很安全,因为我知道,他就在我身边。

The chain of love
爱的延续

You don't owe me a thing, I've been there too. Someone once helped me out the way I'm helping you.

你不欠我什么。我也曾经有过困难，但是有人帮助了我，就像我这样帮助你一样。

What comes around goes around.[1]

He was driving home one evening, on a two-lane country road. Work, in this small mid-western community, was almost as slow as his beat-up[2] Pontiac[3]. But he never quit looking. Ever since the factory closed, he'd been unemployed, and with winter raging on, the chill had finally hit home.

It was a lonely road. Not very many people had a reason to be on it, unless they were leaving. Most of his friends had already left. They had families to feed and dreams to fulfill. But he stayed on. After all, this was where he buried his mother and father. He was born here and knew the country. He could go down this road blind, and tell you what was on either side, and with his headlights[4] not working, that came in handy[5]. It was starting to get dark and light snow flurries were coming down. He'd better get a move on.

You know, he almost didn't see the old lady, stranded[6] on the side of the road. But even in the dim light of day, he could see she needed help. So he pulled up in front of her Mercedes[7] and got out. His Pontiac was still sputtering[8] when he approached her.

Even with the smile on his face, she was worried. No one had stopped to help for the last hour or so. Was he going to hurt her? He didn't look safe, he looked poor and hungry. He could see that she was frightened, standing out there in cold. He knew how she felt. It was that chill that only fear can put in you. He said, "I'm

爱的延续

好心有好报。

傍晚的时候，他驱车回家，行驶在双车道的乡间小路上。在这个中西部的小地方，工作节奏几乎和他的破旧的庞蒂亚克牌车一样慢，但他从未停止过找工作。自从工厂关闭以来，他一直失业。严酷的冬天来了，寒冷侵袭着他的家。

这是一条孤独的路。很少有人会因为什么事而出现在这条路上，除非他们要离开这里。他的朋友大部分已经离开这里了，他们有家要养，有梦想要去实现，但他却留下了。毕竟，他的父母都长眠于此。他出生在这里，熟悉这里的一草一木。他闭着眼都能够顺着这条路走下去，而且还能告诉你路的两边有什么。如果他的前车灯坏了，他的这套本事一定会派上用场。天色渐渐变黑，天上又下着小雪，他必须赶紧回家。

你知道，他几乎没有看到那个被困在路边的老太太。但即使在昏暗的天色下，他也能够看出她需要帮助。于是，他把车停在她的奔驰车前，走了出来。他走向她的时候，他的庞蒂亚克还在噼里啪啦地响着。

尽管他脸上带着微笑，她还是很害怕。在这之前大约一个小时都没有人停下来帮她。他会伤害她吗？他看上去穷困、饥饿，让人

❶ what comes around goes around
好心有好报，善有善报
❷ beat-up
adj. 破旧的
❸ Pontiac
n 一种中低档的汽车品牌
❹ headlight
/ˈhedlaɪt/
n. 汽车的前灯
❺ come in handy
迟早有用，派得上用场
❻ strand
/strænd/
vt. 使陷于困境
❼ Mercedes
n. 梅塞得斯(奔驰)轿车
❽ sputter
/ˈspʌtə/
vi. 发出噼里啪啦的声音

here to help you m'am. Why don't you wait in the car where it's warm. By the way, my name is Joe."

Well, all she had was a flat tire, but for an old lady, that was bad enough. Joe crawled under the car looking for a place to put the jack[9], skinning his knuckles a time or two. Soon he was able to change the tire. But he had to get dirty and his hands hurt. As he was lightening up the lug nuts, she rolled down her window and began to talk to him. She told him that she was from St. Louis and was only just passing through. She couldn't thank him enough for coming to her aid. Joe just smiled. She asked him how much she owed, him. Any amount would have been all right with her. She had already imagined all the awful things that could have happened had he not stopped. Joe never thought twice about the money. This was not a job to him. This was helping someone in need, and God knows there were plenty who had given him a hand in the past. He had lived his whole life that way, and it never occurred to[10] him to act any other way. He told her that if she really wanted to pay him back, the next time she saw someone who needed help, she could give that person the assistance that they needed, and Joe added "...and think of me".

He waited until she started her car and drove off. It had been a cold and depressing day, but he felt good as he headed for home, disappearing into the twilight[11].

A few miles down the road the lady saw a small cafe. She went in to grab a bite to eat, and take the chill off before she

缺乏安全感。她战战兢兢地站在那里,他看出来她害怕了。他知道她的感受,那是一种因为恐惧而使人不寒而栗的感受。他说:"夫人,我是来帮助你的。你为什么不到车子里去等呢?那里暖和一些。顺便说一句,我的名字叫乔。"

她的问题只是轮胎瘪了,但对一个老太太来说可是够糟糕的了。乔爬到车底下,找一个能够放千斤顶的地方,手指关节的皮肤被蹭破了一两处。一会儿功夫,他就开始换轮胎了。他自己弄得脏兮兮的,而且手指也受伤了。他正在拧紧螺母时,她把车窗转下,开始和他说话。她说她从圣路易斯来,正好经过这里。她对他的帮助感激不尽。他只是笑着看了看她。她问要给他多少钱作为酬谢,要多少都没问题。要不是乔停下来帮忙,她想象得出所有会发生的可怕的事情。乔从来没有过多地考虑过钱的事情。这不是他的工作,他是帮助处于困境中的人。上帝知道过去有好多人曾向他伸出过援助之手。这是他做人的一贯作风,从来没有想到过别的做法。他告诉她,如果她真想给他报酬的话,那么在她下次看见需要帮助的人时,就请帮助他人。乔又加了一句:"想想我。"

他一直等到她发动汽车开走。这是一个

⑨ jack
/dʒæk/
n. 千斤顶
⑩ occur to sb.
某人想起
⑪ twilight
/ˈtwaɪlaɪt/
n. 暮色,黄昏

made the last leg[12] of her trip home. It was a dingy looking restaurant. Outside were two old gas pumps. The whole scene was unfamiliar to her. The cash register was like the telephone of an out of work actor —it didn't ring much.

Her waitress came over and brought a clean towel to wipe her wet hair. She had a sweet smile. The lady noticed that the waitress was nearly eight months pregnant, but she never let the strain and aches change her attitude. The old lady wondered how someone who had so little could be so giving[13] to a stranger. Then she remembered Joe.

After the lady finished her meal, and the waitress went to get her change for a hundred dollar bill, the lady slipped right out the door. She was gone by the time the waitress came back. She wondered where the lady could be, then she noticed something written on the napkin under which were 4 more $100 bills.

There were tears in her eyes, when she read what the lady had written. It said, "You don't owe me a thing, I've been there too. Someone once helped me out the way I'm helping you. If you really want to pay me back, here's what you do. Don't let the chain of love end with you."

Well, there were tables to clear, sugar bowls to fill, and people to serve, but the waitress made it through another day. That night when she got home from work and climbed into bed, she was thinking about the money and what the lady had written. How

寒冷而且阴沉的日子,但他在回家的路上感觉很好。渐渐地,他消失在暮色中。

那位女士顺着路走了几英里后,看到了一家小咖啡馆。她走进去匆匆地凑合着吃了点东西,以便去掉身上的寒气然后踏上返乡的最后征程。这是一家看上去很邋遢的餐馆,外面有两个旧的气泵。这一切对她来说都不熟悉。这里的收银机,就如同一个失了业的演员的电话机一样很少使用。

服务员走了过来,拿着一条干净的毛巾把她的头发擦干。她笑得很甜。这位女士注意到服务员已有大约8个月的身孕了,但是她没有因为疲劳和疼痛改变对客人的态度。这位老太太非常惊讶:一个如此贫苦的人何以能如此乐于付出?这时,她想起了乔。

吃完饭后,当女服务员给她的100美元找零钱的时候,这位女士悄悄地溜出了门。服务员回来的时候,她已经不知去向了。服务员正在疑惑那位女士去了哪里,这时她看到桌子上有一张纸巾上面写着什么,底下还放着4张百元大钞。

她看到那位女士写的话后,热泪盈眶。纸条上写道:"你不欠我什么。我也曾经有过困难,但是有人帮助了我,就像我这样帮助你一样。如果你真的想感谢我,那么你也

⑫ **leg**
/leg/
n.(旅程或赛程的)一段

⑬ **giving**
/ˈɡɪvɪŋ/
adj. 乐于付出的

could she have known how much she and her husband needed it?. With the baby due next month, it was going to be hard. She knew how worried her husband was, and as he lay sleeping next to her, she gave him a soft kiss and whispered soft and low, "Everything's gonna be all right; I love you, Joe."

应该这样做。让爱永远在世间延续下去！"

　　这位服务员还要擦桌子，装糖碗，为客人服务，但她终于又挺过了一天。当她晚上下班回家上床睡觉的时候，她想起了那些钱和老妇人写的东西。她怎么知道她和她丈夫那么需要钱呢？下个月孩子就要临产了，他俩的处境会非常艰难。她知道她的丈夫有多么着急，此刻他就在她身边熟睡。她轻轻地亲了他一下，低声道："一切都会好的，我爱你，乔。"

Those strangers we know
熟悉的陌生人

I began to realize that a significant part of our daily life consists of such encounters with familiar strangers.

我开始意识到，平时经常遇到的那些熟悉的陌生人构成了我们日常生活很重要的一部分。

We may look at the world around us, but somehow we manage not to see it until whatever it is we've become accustomed to suddenly disappears. Take, for example, the neatly attired[1] woman I used to see—or look at —on my way to work each morning.

For three years, no matter what the weather, she was always waiting at the bus stop around 8 a.m. On snowy days, she wore heavy boots and a woolen scarf. Summer time brought out neat, belted cotton dresses and a straw hat worn low over her eyeglasses. Clearly a working woman, she exuded[2] an air of competence, stability and dependability.

Of course, I remembered all this only after she vanished. It was then I realized how much I counted on seeing her each morning. You might say I missed her.

Naturally, I had fantasies about her disappearance. Accident? Something worse? Now that she was gone, I felt I had known her.

I began to realize that a significant part of our daily life consists of such encounters with familiar strangers: the power walker you see every afternoon at three o'clock. The woman who regularly walks her Yorkie at the crack of dawn. The dapper[3] twin brothers you see at the library.

Such people are important markers in the landscape of our lives. They add weight to our sense of place and belonging.

熟悉的陌生人

我们每天都注视着周围的世界，但是，只有那些我们习以为常的东西突然消失了的时候，我们才会真正注意到这个世界。正像我早已习惯每天早上上班时，注意到，确切地说是看到，那位衣着整洁的女士。

三年来，不管天气如何，早上8点钟左右，总能看到她在车站等车。冬天，她穿着厚的皮靴，裹着羊毛围巾；夏日，则是一身得体的束腰棉质女装，一顶草帽低低地遮过眼镜。很显然，她是一位职业女性，通身都显得干练、沉着和可靠。

当然，仅仅在她消失之后，我才形成了对她的记忆。直到那时，我才意识到，每天早上我多么渴望能见到她，甚至可以说，我有点儿想她。

对于她的消失，我不免胡思乱想。是因为意外的事故？还是更糟的事情？现在她消失了，我才感觉到很早以前自己就已经认识她了。

我开始意识到，平时经常遇到的那些熟悉的陌生人构成了我们日常生活很重要的一部分：每天下午三点，那个走路风风火火的行人；每天破晓时，那个牵着长毛小狗散步的女人；还有图书馆里那一对风度翩翩的孪生兄弟。

❶ **attire**
/ə'taɪə/
v.穿着，盛装

❷ **exude**
/ɪg'zju:d/
v. 流出；溢出

❸ **dapper**
/'dæpə/
adj.衣冠楚楚的；风度翩翩的

Think about it. If, while walking to work, we mark where we are by passing a certain building, why should we not mark where we are when we pass a familiar, though unnamed, person?

After all, if part of being a tourist is seeing nothing and no-one familiar to you, then can we not say that seeing the familiar jogger[4] or shopper is part of what makes us citizens of our community?

This is one thing an immigrant longs for, I suppose: the sight of the familiar stranger. The shopkeeper who nods[5] to you. The bus driver who drives you to work each day. The woman you see walking her child to school.

Sometimes I wonder: am I a familiar stranger to someone?

Perhaps a shopper at the supermarket sees me there every Saturday without really noting my presence[6]. Or maybe someone at the drugstore counter where I eat breakfast would notice if I stopped showing up.

Once in a while you might actually meet one of these familiar strangers, as I did a few months ago. I was standing in a coffee shop when a woman said hello. "Do you know who I am?" she asked. And I did. She was a patient I had seen many times in my doctor's office. We had an easy, familiar chat—although we never got around to exchanging names.

正是这些人使我们的生活具体起来,是他们使我们更强烈地意识到一种方位感和归属感。

想想吧,我们走路上班时,会把途经的建筑物作为线路的标志。那么为什么我们不能把经常遇到的一个熟悉的、虽然叫不上名字的人作为线路的标志呢?

如果说旅行者生活的一部分就是碰不到一个熟悉的事物,见不到一个熟悉的人。那么我们为什么不能说,作为社区的成员,我们生活的一部分就是看到那些熟悉的慢跑者或购物者呢?

我想一个刚迁入此地的外乡人,渴望看到的就是这样一些熟悉的陌生人:那个向你点头问候的店主,那个每天开车载你上下班的公共汽车司机,还有那个每天送孩子上学的母亲。

有时我会想:是不是在别人眼里,我也是个熟悉的陌生人呢?

或许购物的顾客每周六也在超市看到了我,却不会真正注意到我。或者在我每天吃早餐的小卖店,柜台后的某个人会注意到我不再光顾那儿了。

偶尔,你也许会和某个熟悉的陌生人有所来往,就像我在几个月前那样。那次,我

❹ **jogger**
/ˈdʒɒɡə/
n. 慢跑者

❺ **nod**
/nɒd/
v. 点头

❻ **presence**
/ˈprezns/
n. 在场

But here's what I remember most about the importance of familiar strangers. Once, driving home from the airport after a long vacation, I was feeling disoriented[4], out-of-place[5]. Then I saw him —the gentleman in the tweed[6] jacket and green cap. I'd seen this man walking through my neighborhood a thousand times.

Ah, I thought, seeing the familiar stranger, I'm home at last.

正在一家咖啡馆里站着,有位女士过来冲我打招呼。她问我,"你知道我是谁吗?"我知道她是谁。她也是一个病人,我在诊所里曾多次见到过。虽然自始至终没有交换彼此的姓名,我们却聊得轻松、亲切。

下面这个例子我认为最能体现熟悉的陌生人的重要性。有一次,在结束了长长的假期之后,我从机场驾车回家,一路上总感觉自己有点儿迷失方向、找不到回家的感觉。忽然,我看到了他——那位身穿花呢夹克,头戴绿色帽子的绅士——我曾经千百次地看到他在这附近走过。

见到了这个熟悉的陌生人,我想,哦,我终于到家了。

❼ disoriented
/dɪsˈɔːrɪentɪd/
adj. 迷失方向的
❽ out-of-place
不在适当的位置上
❾ tweed
/twiːd/
n. 粗花呢

Paradox of our times
我们这个时代的尴尬

We've learned how to make a living, but not a life; we've added years to life, not life to years.

我们掌握了谋生手段,却不懂得生活真谛;我们把年华付诸流水,却不曾将生命倾注其中。

We have bigger houses and smaller families; more conveniences, but less time; we have more degrees, but less common sense; more knowledge, but less judgment; more experts, but more problems; more medicine, but less wellness.

We spend too recklessly[1], laugh too little, drive too fast, get to angry too quickly, stay up too late, get up too tired, read too little, watch TV too often, and pray too seldom. We have multiplied our possessions, but reduced our values. We talk too much, love too little and lie too often. We've learned how to make a living, but not a life; we've added years to life, not life to years.

We have taller buildings, but shorter tempers; wider freeways, but narrower viewpoints. We spend more, but have less; we buy more, but enjoy it less.

We've been all the way to the moon and back, but have trouble crossing the street to meet the new neighbor. We've conquered outer space, but not inner space. We've split the atom, but not our prejudice[2]; we write more, but learn less; plan more, but accomplish less.

We've learned to rush, but not to wait; we have higher incomes, but lower morals. We build more computers to hold more information, to produce more copies, but have less communication. We are long on quantity, but short on quality.

These are the times of fast foods and slow digestion[3]; tall

我们这个时代的尴尬

　　我们居住的房屋越来越宽敞，家庭却越来越小型化；可以享受的生活便利日益增多，属于自己的时间却日趋减少；我们获得了一张又一张学位证书，却愈加频繁地陷入对常识的茫然中；我们广泛地涉猎各类知识，却越来越缺乏对于外界事物的准确把握和判断；专家越来越多，问题却也日渐增加；药物越吃越多，健康却每况愈下。

　　我们花钱太疯，笑容太少，开车太快，发怒太急，熬夜太晚，起身太累，文章读得太少，电视看得太勤，祷告做得太少。

　　我们不断聚敛物质财富，却逐渐丢失了自我价值。我们的话语太多，真爱太少，谎言泛滥。我们掌握了谋生手段，却不懂得生活真谛；我们让年华付诸流水，却不曾将生命倾注其中。

　　我们的住房越来越好，脾气却越来越糟；我们行驶的道路越来越宽阔，眼光却越来越狭隘。我们付出很多，可获得的很少；我们购买了很多，可从中得到的乐趣却很少。

　　我们能够往返于地球与月球之间，却不乐于穿过马路向新邻居问好。我们可以征服太空，却慑于走进内心世界。我们可以分裂原子，却不能突破思想偏见；我们写得很多，可学到的很少；计划很多，可完成的很少。

❶ **recklessly**
/ˈreklɪslɪ/
adv. 鲁莽地，不顾一切地

❷ **prejudice**
/ˈpredʒʊdɪs/
n. 偏见，成见

❸ **digestion**
/dɪˈdʒestʃən/
n. 消化

men and short character; steep[4] profits and shallow relationships. More leisure and less fun; more kinds of food, but less nutrition[5]; two incomes, but more divorce; fancier houses, but broken homes.

我们学会了追赶时间，却没学会耐心等待；我们拥有的财富越来越多，道德品质却日益沦丧。我们生产更多的电脑用于存储更多的信息和制造更多的拷贝，而相互间的交流与沟通却越来越少。我们拥有的是数量，缺乏的是质量。

这是一个快餐食品和消化迟缓相伴的时代；一个体格高大和性格病态并存的时代；一个追名逐利和人情冷漠相生的时代。我们的休闲多了，乐趣却少了；食品种类多了，营养却少了；双薪家庭增加了，离婚率也激升了；居室的装修华丽了，家庭却残缺破碎了。

❹ **steep**
/stiːp/
adj. 过高的，过分的

❺ **nutrition**
/njuːˈtrɪʃn/
n. 营养

The Teddy Stoddard's story
泰迪·斯托达德的故事

You never can tell what type of impact you may make on another's life by your actions or lack of action. Consider this fact in your venture through life.

你永远不会知道,你的一言一行,一举一动会对他人的生活产生多大的影响。一生都记住这一点吧。

Jean Thompson stood in front of her fifth-grade class on the very first day of school in the fall and told the children a lie.

Like most teachers, she looked at her pupils and said that she loved them all the same, that she would treat them all alike. And that was impossible because there in front of her, slumped[1] in his seat on the third row, was a little boy named Teddy Stoddard.

Mrs. Thompson had watched Teddy the year before and noticed he didn't play well with the other children, that his clothes were unkempt[2] and that he constantly needed a bath. And Teddy was unpleasant.

It got to the point during the first few months that she would actually take delight in marking his papers with a broad red pen, making bold X's and then marking the F at the top of the paper, biggest of all.

Because Teddy was a sullen little boy, no one else seemed to enjoy him, either.

At the school where Mrs. Thompson taught, she was required to review each child's records and put Teddy's off until last. When she opened his file, she was in for a surprise. His first-grade teacher wrote, "Teddy is a bright, inquisitive[3] child with a ready laugh. He does his work neatly and has good manners...he is a joy to be around."

秋季开学的头一天，琼·汤普森在她即将执教的五年级学生面前撒了个谎。像所有老师一样，她注视着她的学生，说她爱他们，不偏不倚，平等对待每一个人。但这是不可能的。就在她面前的第三排，一个叫泰迪·斯托达德的小男孩无精打采地斜靠在座位上。

汤普森夫人前一年里曾留心观察过这个孩子，发现他和其他的孩子玩不到一块儿，还穿着邋遢，老不洗澡。总之，泰迪不讨人喜欢。

头几个月，汤普森夫人发现，泰迪的作业差得都让人发笑。她用粗粗的红笔，在他作业上打上一个个醒目的红叉，然后在作业上方写上最大号的"不及格"。

正是因为泰迪抑郁的性格，好像也没别的什么人喜欢他。

汤普森夫人任教的学校要求她重新审读孩子们的履历，她把泰迪的放在了最后一个。翻到泰迪的档案时，她吃了一惊。一年级老师这样评价他，"泰迪聪明伶俐，勤学好问，开朗爱笑。作业整齐工整，待人礼貌和气……他处处给人带来欢乐。"

二年级老师写道，"泰迪是个深受同学喜爱的优秀学生，但他因母亲身患绝症而忧虑重重。他家的生活肯定十分艰难。"

❶ **slump**
/slʌmp/
v. 颓然倒下，突然落下

❷ **unkempt**
/ʌnˈkempt/
adj. 不整洁的，邋遢的

❸ **inquisitive**
/ɪnˈkwɪzɪtɪv/
adj. 好问的，好追根究底的

His second-grade teacher wrote, "Teddy is an excellent student well-liked by his classmates, but he is troubled because his mother has a terminal[4] illness and life at home must be a struggle."

His third-grade teacher wrote, "Teddy continues to work hard but his mother's death has been hard on him. He tries to do his best but his father doesn't show much interest and his home life will soon affect him if some steps aren't taken."

Teddy's fourth-grade teacher wrote, "Teddy is withdrawn[5] and doesn't show much interest in school. He doesn't have many friends and sometimes sleeps in class. He is tardy[6] and could become a problem."

By now Mrs. Thompson realized the problem but Christmas was coming fast. It was all she could do, with the school play and all, until the day before the holidays began and she was suddenly forced to focus on Teddy Stoddard.

Her children brought her presents, all in beautiful ribbon and bright paper, except for Teddy's, which was clumsily wrapped in the heavy, brown paper of a scissored grocery bag. Mrs. Thompson took pains to open it in the middle of the other presents. Some of the children started to laugh when she found a rhinestone[7] bracelet[8] with some of the stones missing, and a bottle that was one-quarter full of cologne[9].

三年级老师的评语是，"泰迪学习依旧十分刻苦，但他母亲的去世对他打击很大。他努力想做到最好，但他父亲对他不大关心。如果不采取措施，他的家庭情况很快就会影响他的学习。"

泰迪四年级老师的话是，"泰迪性格内向，对功课兴趣不大。他朋友不多，上课有时睡觉，做事拖沓，将来会是个难管教的孩子。"

此刻，汤普森夫人已明白问题出在哪里了。可圣诞节很快就要到了，学校有各种活动，她无暇他顾。到了假日的前一天，她没料到有件事让自己不得不把注意力转移到泰达·斯托达德身上。

那天学生给她带来了各种各样的礼物，礼物上都扎着漂亮的绸带，裹着鲜亮的彩纸，只有泰迪的礼物不大一样，用一块从杂货店袋子上剪下的棕色厚纸笨拙地包着，汤普森夫人费了好大劲儿才把它打开。里面是一串莱茵石手链，其中几颗已经掉了，还有一瓶仅剩四分之一的古龙香水，有些孩子见了不禁笑出声来。

她却赞叹说，多漂亮的手链啊，说着把手链戴上，并在另一只手腕上搭了些古龙香水。这止住了孩子们的笑声。泰迪·斯托达德

❹ **terminal**
/'tɜːmɪnəl/
adj. (病症)不治的，致命的；晚期的

❺ **withdrawn**
/wɪð'drɔːn/
adj. 孤僻的，离群的，内向的

❻ **tardy**
/'tɑːdɪ/
adj. 行动缓慢的，拖拖拉拉的

❼ **rhinestone**
/'raɪnstəʊn/
n. 莱茵石

❽ **bracelet**
/'breɪslɪt/
n. 手链

❾ **cologne**
/kə'ləʊn/
n. 古龙香水

She stifled[10] the children's laughter when she exclaimed how pretty the bracelet was, putting it on, and dabbing[11] some of the perfume behind the other wrist. Teddy Stoddard stayed behind just long enough to say, "Mrs. Thompson, today you smelled just like my mom used to."

After the children left, she cried for at least an hour.

On that very day, she quit teaching reading, writing and speaking. Instead, she began to teach children. Jean Thompson paid particular attention to one they all called "Teddy."

As she worked with him, his mind seemed to come alive. The more she encouraged him, the faster he responded. On days there would be an important test, Mrs. Thompson would remember that cologne. By the end of the year he had become one of the smartest children in the class and...well, he had also become the "pet" of the teacher who had once vowed to love all of her children exactly the same.

A year later she found a note under her door, from Teddy, telling her that of all the teachers he'd had in elementary school, she was his favorite.

Six years went by before she got another note from Teddy. He then wrote that he had finished high school, third in his class, and she was still his favorite teacher of all time.

只是说了一句，"汤普森夫人，今天你身上的味道和我妈妈过去一样。"

孩子们离开后，她哭了足足一个钟头。

从那天起，她不再简单地教学生读书、写字、说话，她开始真正意义地教育学生。她还特别关注一个大家都叫他"泰迪"的学生。

每当汤普森夫人帮助泰迪学习时，他的思维似乎变得活跃了。她给他的鼓励越多，他的反应就越快。每逢有重要的考试，汤普森夫人总不忘那古龙香水。到了年底，泰迪一跃成为班上最聪颖出色的孩子之一。当然，他也成了那位曾发誓说她会毫无二致地爱每个学生的老师的宠儿。

一年过后，她在门下发现了一张纸条。纸条是泰迪写的，说她是小学所有老师中他最喜欢的一个。

又过了6年，她又收到泰迪的一张纸条。说他已读完中学，名列全班第三，而她依然是他最喜欢的老师。

又过了4年，她收到泰迪的一封信，说虽然有时也觉得很艰难，但他一直坚持上学读书，即将以最优异的成绩从大学毕业。他向汤普森夫人保证说她依然是他最喜欢的老师。

又是6个年头过去了，泰迪又来了一封

⓵ **stifle**
/ˈstaɪfl/
vt. 阻止，抑止

⓶ **dab**
/dæb/
vt. 搽，抹

Four years after that, she got another letter, saying that while things had been tough[12] at times, he'd stayed in school, had stuck with it, and would graduate from college with the highest of honors. He assured Mrs. Thompson she was still his favorite teacher.

Then six more years passed and yet another letter came. This time he explained that after he got his bachelor's degree, he decided to go a little further. The letter explained that she was still his favorite teacher but that now his name was a little longer. The letter was signed Theodore F. Stoddard, M.D.

The story doesn't end there. You see, there was yet another letter that Spring Teddy said he'd met this girl and was to be married. He explained that his father had died a couple of years ago and he was wondering...well, if Mrs. Thompson might agree to sit in the pew[13] usually reserved for the mother of the groom.

And guess what, she wore that bracelet, the rhinestones missing. And I bet on that special day, Jean Thompson smelled just like, well, just like the way Teddy remembered his mother smelling on their last Christmas together.

信。这一次,他写道他获得学士学位后,决定再上一层楼。信中说她依旧是他最喜欢的老师,但现在他的名字长了些。署名是医学博士西奥多·F·斯托达德。

故事还没完。要知道,那年春天泰迪又来了一封信,说他遇到了一个女孩,准备结婚了。他说他的父亲几年前过世了,他想知道,嗯,汤普森夫人是否愿意出席婚礼并在教堂中坐在新郎母亲的位置。

你能猜出当天汤普森夫人戴上那串缺了几颗莱茵石手链时的情形吗?我敢说在那个婚礼上汤普森夫人的味道就像泰迪母亲和泰迪最后一次共度圣诞节时的味道一模一样。

⑫ **tough**
/tʌf/
adj. 困难的
⑬ **pew**
/pju:/
n. (教堂里)有靠背的长椅

Choose optimism
选择乐观

When the world is seen as a hopeful, positive place, people are empowered to attempt and to achieve.

当人们把世界看作一个光明与希望之地,他们将被赋予努力进取和成就事业的力量。

If you expect something to turn out badly, it probably will. Pessimism is seldom disappointed. But the same principle also works in reverse[1]. If you expect good things to happen, they usually do! There seems to be a natural cause-and-effect relationship between optimism and success.

Optimism and pessimism are both powerful forces, and each of us must choose which we want to shape our outlook and our expectations. There is enough good and bad in everyone's life—ample sorrow and happiness, sufficient joy and pain —to find a rational basis for either optimism or pessimism. We can choose to laugh or cry, bless or curse. It's our decision: From which perspective do we want to view life? Will we look up in hope or down in despair?

I believe in the upward look. I choose to highlight[2] the positive and slip right over the negative. I am an optimist by choice as much as by nature. Sure, I know that sorrow exists. I am in my 70s now, and I've lived through more than one crisis. But when all is said and done, I find that the good in life far outweighs[3] the bad.

An optimistic attitude is not a luxury; it's a necessity. The way you look at life will determine how you feel, how you perform, and how well you will get along with other people. Conversely, negative thoughts, attitudes, and expectations feed on themselves; they become a self-fulfilling prophecy. Pessimism creates a dismal place where no one wants to live.

选择乐观

假如你预期某事会有不妙的结果，结局也许就真的不妙——悲观的想法很少落空。但这个法则反过来也同样成立：如果你自感鸿运当头，通常就会有好运降临！在乐观与成功之间似乎有一种天然的因果关系。

乐观和悲观都是强大的力量，我们每个人都必须在这两者之间做出选择，从而给我们对未来的展望和预期染上或明或暗的色彩。每个人的生命中都有足够多的幸与不幸——数不清的哀伤和喜悦、欢欣与痛苦——给我们乐观或悲观的理由。我们可以选择哭或是笑、祝福或是诅咒。我们可以选择用什么样的眼光去看待生活——是昂首寻找希望抑或垂头在绝望中逡巡。

我喜欢向上看。我会把注意力集中在生活中光明的一面，忽略那些阴暗的角落。天性和个人选择使我成了一个乐观主义者。当然，我知道生命中总有伤痛，年逾古稀的我曾不止一次经历过危机。但是，当一切尘埃落定，我发现生命中的美好远远比丑恶要多。

乐观的态度不是一种奢侈品；它是我们生活的必需。你看待生活的方式将决定你的感受、你的表现，以及你与他人相处得怎样。反过来，悲观的想法、态度和预期也会自成因果；它们是能自我实现的预言。悲观会制

❶ **in reverse**
相反，反过来
❷ **highlight**
/'haɪlaɪt/
vt. 使注意力集中于
❸ **outweigh**
/aʊt'weɪ/
vt. 比…更重要，超过

Years ago, I drove into a service station to get some gas. It was a beautiful day, and I was feeling great. As I walked into the station to pay for the gas, the attendant said to me, "How do you feel?" That seemed like an odd question, but I felt fine and told him so. "You don't look well," he replied. This took me completely by surprise. A little less confidently, I told him that I had never felt better. Without hesitation, he continued to tell me how bad I looked and that my skin appeared yellow.

By the time I left the service station, I was feeling a little uneasy. About a block away, I pulled over to the side of the road to look at my face in the mirror. How did I feel? Was I jaundiced[4]? Was everything all right? By the time I got home, I was beginning to feel a little queasy[5]. Did I have a bad liver? Had I picked up some rare disease?

The next time I went into that gas station, feeling fine again, I figured out what had happened. The place had recently been painted a bright, bilious[6] yellow, and the light reflecting off the walls made everyone inside look as though they had hepatitis[7]! I wondered how many other folks had reacted the way I did. I had let one short conversation with a total stranger change my attitude for an entire day. He told me I looked sick, and before long, I was actually feeling sick. That single negative observation had a profound effect on the way I felt and acted.

The only thing more powerful than negativism is a positive affirmation[8], a word of optimism and hope. One of the things I am

造出无人愿往的黑暗处所。

几年前,我驱车去一个加油站加油。那天天气很好,我的心情也不错。当我走进加油站付油钱时,服务员问我:"你感觉怎样?"问题问得有点古怪,我感觉很好,于是便照实回答了他。他又说:"你气色不好。"他的话让我非常吃惊。我告诉他我的感觉从未像现在这么好,但说此话时已不像原来那么底气十足。而他则毫无顾忌地继续大讲我的气色是如何的差劲,还说我肤色发黄。

在离开加油站的时候,我觉得有点心神不宁。驶出一个街区之后,我把车泊在路旁,从镜中审视自己的脸。我怎么了?我得了黄疸病吗?是不是有什么异常?等我回到家里,我开始觉得有点恶心。我的肝脏出了毛病吗?是不是染上了什么怪病?

再次光顾那个加油站的时候,我已恢复正常,感觉良好,而且明白了个中蹊跷。这个地方不久前把墙漆上了一种鲜亮的,胆汁般的黄色,这颜色使置身其中的每一个人都被映得像得了肝炎。不知道有多少人也曾有过和我相似的经历。和一个完全陌生的人的一次短短的对话竟然改变了我整整一天的心情。他说我面有病容,很快我就真的觉得不舒服了,仅仅是一个消极的看法就大大影响

❹ **jaundiced**
/ˈdʒɔːndɪst/
adj. 患黄疸的

❺ **queasy**
/ˈkwiːzɪ/
adj. 恶心的,想吐的

❻ **bilious**
/ˈbɪlɪəs/
adj. 胆汁病的

❼ **hepatitis**
/ˌhepəˈtaɪtɪs/
n. 肝炎

❽ **affirmation**
/ˌæfəˈmeɪʃn/
n. 肯定,确认

most thankful for is the fact that I have grown up in a nation with a grand tradition of optimism. When a whole culture adopts an upward look, incredible things can be accomplished. When the world is seen as a hopeful, positive place, people are empowered to attempt and to achieve.

Optimism doesn't need to be naive. We can be an optimist and still recognize that problems exist and that some of them are not dealt with easily. But what a difference optimism makes in the attitude of the problem solver! Optimism diverts[9] our attention away from negativism and channels it into positive, constructive thinking. When you're an optimist, you're more concerned with problem-solving than with useless carping[10] about issues. In fact, without optimism, issues as big and ongoing[11] as poverty have no hope of solution. It takes a dreamer—someone with hopelessly optimistic ideas, great persistence, and unlimited confidence—to tackle a problem that big. It's your choice.

了我感觉和行为的方式。

惟一比否定态度更有力量的是一个积极的肯定，一句充满乐观与希望的话语。最让我心存感激的事情之一就是我生长在一个有着光荣的乐观主义传统的国度。当一种文化从整体上采取了一种积极向上的态度，不可思议的事情也能变成现实。当人们把世界看作一个光明与希望之地，他们将被赋予努力进取和成就事业的力量。

乐观并不意味着幼稚。在保持乐观的同时，我们仍然能意识到问题的存在，意识到有些问题非常棘手。乐观带来的改变在于面对问题的态度。乐观精神使我们的注意力从消极的否定态度转向积极的、建设性的思考。乐观主义者更关心如何解决问题，而不是毫无意义的怨天尤人。说真的，如果没有乐观精神，像贫穷这样沉重且持续存在的问题是无望解决的。解决这样的问题需要一个梦想家——一个拥有九死不悔的乐观、矢志不移的坚韧和无限信心的人。何去何从，由你决定。

❾ **divert**
/daɪˈvɜːt/
v. (+from) 使(人)分心；转移(注意力)

❿ **carp**
/kɑːp/
v. 挑剔，吹毛求疵

⓫ **ongoing**
/ˈɒnˌɡəʊɪŋ/
adj. 不断前进(发展)中的，继续进行的

The wholeness of life
健全的人生

There is a wholeness about the person who has come to terms with his limitations, who has been brave enough to let go of his unrealistic dreams and not feel like a failure for doing so.

人生的完整性在于知道如何面对缺陷，如何勇敢地摒弃不现实的幻想而又不以此为憾。

Once a circle missed a wedge[1]. The circle wanted to be whole, so it went around looking for its missing piece. But because it was incomplete and therefore could roll only very slowly, it admired the flowers along the way. It chatted with worms. It enjoyed the sunshine. It found lots of different pieces, but none of them fit. So it left them all by the side of the road and kept on searching. Then one day the circle found a piece that fit perfectly. It was so happy. Now it could be whole, with nothing missing. It incorporated[2] the missing piece into itself and began to roll. Now that it was a perfect circle, it could roll very fast, too fast to notice flowers or talk to the worms. When it realized how different the world seemed when it rolled so quickly, it stopped, left its found piece by the side of the road and rolled slowly away.

The lesson of the story, I suggested, was that in some strange sense we are more whole when we are missing something. The man who has everything is in some ways a poor man. He will never know what it feels like to yearn, to hope, to nourish[3] his soul with the dream of something better. He will never know the experience of having someone who loves him give him something he has always wanted or never had.

There is a wholeness about the person who has come to terms with his limitations, who has been brave enough to let go of his unrealistic dreams and not feel like a failure for doing so. There is a wholeness about the man or woman who has learned that he or she is strong enough to go through a tragedy and survive, she can lose someone and still feel like a complete person.

从前，一个圆圈缺了一块楔子。它想保持完整，便四处寻找那块楔子。由于不完整，所以它只能慢慢地滚动。一路上，它对花儿露出羡慕之色。它与蠕虫聊天。它还享受到了阳光。圆圈找到了许多不同的楔子，但没有一件与它相配。所以，它将它们统统弃置路旁，继续寻觅。终于有一天，它找到了一个完美的配件。圆圈特别高兴，现在它可以说是完美无缺了。它装好配件，并开始滚动起来。现在它已成了一个完美的圆圈，所以滚动得非常快，以至于难以观赏花儿，也无暇与蠕虫倾诉心声。当圆圈意识到因为快速的滚动它失去了原有的世界时，它不禁停了下来，将找到的配件弃置路旁，又开始慢慢地滚动。

我觉得这个故事告诉我们，从某种奇妙的意义上讲，当我们失去了一些东西时反而更加完整。一个拥有一切的人其实在某些方面是个穷人。他永远也体会不到什么是渴望、期待及如何用美好梦想滋养自己的灵魂。他也永远不会有这样一种体验：一个爱他的人送给他某种他梦寐以求的或者从未拥有过的东西意味着什么。

人生的完整性在于知道如何面对缺陷；如何勇敢地摒弃不现实的幻想而又不以此为

❶ **wedge**
/wedʒ/
n. 楔，楔形物
❷ **incorporate**
/ɪnˈkɔːpəreɪt/
vt. 结合，合并
❸ **nourish**
/ˈnʌrɪʃ/
vt. 使滋养，使健壮

Life is not a trap set for us by God so that he can condemn[4] us for failing. Life is not a <u>spelling bee</u>[5], where no matter how many words you've gotten right, you're disqualified[6] if you make one mistake. Life is more like a baseball season, where even the best team loses one third of its games and even the worst team has its days of brilliance. Our goal is to win more games than we lose.

When we accept that imperfection[7] is part of being human, and when we can continue rolling through life and appreciate it, we will have achieved a wholeness that others can only aspire to. That, I believe, is what God asks of us—not "Be perfect", not "Don't even make a mistake", but "Be whole".

憾。人生的完整性还在于学会勇敢面对人生悲剧而继续生存，能够在失去亲人后依然表现出完整的个人风范。

　　人生不是上帝为谴责我们的缺陷而给我们布下的陷阱。人生也不是一场拼字游戏比赛，不管你拼出多少单词，一旦出现了一个错误，你便前功尽弃。人生更像是一个棒球赛季，即使最好的球队也会输掉1/3的比赛，而最差的球队也有春风得意的日子。我们的目标就是多赢球，少输球。当我们接受不完整性是人类本性的一部分，当我们不断地进行人生滚动并能欣赏其价值时，我们就会获得其他人仅能渴望的完整人生。我相信这就是上帝对我们的要求：不求"完美"，也不求"永不犯错误"，而是求得人生的"完整"。

❹ **condemn**
/kən'dem/
vt. 谴责，强烈指责

❺ **spelling bee**
（小学生等的）拼字比赛

❻ **disqualify**
/dɪs'kwɒlɪfaɪ/
vt. 使不合格，使无资格

❼ **imperfection**
/ˌɪmpə'fekʃn/
n. 不完美性，有缺陷性

图书在版编目（CIP）数据

英汉对照·心灵阅读. 1, 人生篇/许兰贞编译. —北京：外文出版社，2004
ISBN 7-119-03727-7

Ⅰ. 英… Ⅱ. 许… Ⅲ. 英语-对照读物-英、汉 Ⅳ. H319.4

中国版本图书馆 CIP 数据核字（2004）第 057272 号

```
外文出版社网址：
    http://www.flp.com.cn
外文出版社电子信箱：
    info@flp.com.cn
    sales@flp.com.cn
```

英汉对照·心灵阅读（一）

人 生 篇

编　译 许兰贞
审　校 林　立

责任编辑 王　蕊　相　永
封面设计 张　蕾
印刷监制 张国祥
出版发行 外文出版社
社　　址 北京市百万庄大街 24 号　　邮政编码　100037
电　　话 （010）68995963/6075（编辑部）
　　　　　　（010）68329514/68327211（推广发行部）
印　　刷 北京中印联印务有限公司
经　　销 新华书店/外文书店
开　　本 大 32 开　　　　　　　　　　字　数　150 千字
印　　数 10001-15000 册　　　　　　印　张　8.625
版　　次 2005 年 4 月第 1 版第 2 次印刷
装　　别 平
书　　号 ISBN 7-119-03727-7/H·1614（外）
定　　价 15.80 元

版权所有　侵权必究